Praise for Living the Faery Life

"Charming, magical, absolutely enchanting, *Living the Faery Life* is a handbook for understanding the origins of the faery people, where they came from and how they are still present in our world today."

—Amy Leigh Mercree, holistic health expert and bestselling author of fifteen books, including *A Little Bit of Goddess*, *The Mood Book: Crystals, Oils, and Rituals to Elevate Your Spirit*, and *100 Days to Calm: A Journal for Finding Everyday Tranquility*

"*Living the Faery Life* is an enchanting introduction to the magical world of fae. Kac Young begins by exploring the fascinating historical contexts of fairies while sharing her own remarkable experiences with the little people. She provides practical guidelines to communing and connecting with the mystical beings on multidimensional levels, and her reverence for the unseen realm is a beautiful reminder there is more to reality than meets the eye.

"This work is as much a gift as it is a guide. Readers worldwide will be crafting fairy gardens, creating fairy doors, and welcoming wonders from otherworldly reaches. In the words of Roald Dahl, 'those who don't believe in magic will never find it.' Kac inspires readers of every age to embrace the world of fairies and invite the magic of nature into their lives."

—Anam Cara Cat, author of *How to Be a Fairy*

T0124599

"Fairies are all around us and Kac's book shows how to bring their special magic into your life."

—Cerridwen Greenleaf

"Kac Young reminds us of something we are in need of in our brash world: the sensitive and delicate nature of fairies and the importance of approaching nature on nature's terms. She also reminds us of their capriciousness and how they are of the wilderness at heart and live by their own laws, which we fare best by well knowing! This book will teach you what you need to know to understand the magical and mysterious ways of fairy folk."

—Elaine Clayton, author of *A Little Bit of Fairies and Making Marks: Discover the Art of Intuitive Drawing*

Living the Faery Life

Living the Faery Life

A Guide to Connecting
with the Magic, Power, and Joy
of the Enchanted Realm

By Kac Young PhD, ND, DCH

CORAL GABLES

Published by Mango Publishing Group, a division of Mango Media Inc.

Cover, Layout & Design: Morgane Leoni
Cover Photo: © A-Star / Shutterstock

For permission requests, please contact the publisher at:

Mango Publishing Group
2850 S Douglas Road, 2nd Floor
Coral Gables, FL 33134 USA
info@mango.bz

For special orders, quantity sales, course adoptions and corporate sales, please email the publisher at sales@mango.bz. For trade and wholesale sales, please contact Ingram Publisher Services at: customer.service@ingramcontent.com or +1.800.509.4887.

Living the Faery Life: A Guide to Connecting with the Magic, Power, and Joy of the Enchanted Realm

Library of Congress Cataloging-in-Publication number: 2019944431
ISBN: (p) 978-1-64250-061-5, (e) 978-1-64250-062-2
BISAC category code: OCC028000, BODY, MIND & SPIRIT / Magick Studies

Printed in the United States of America

To Helen Keller Squirrel

One of the greatest faeries I ever had
the pleasure of meeting

And as the seasons come and go, here's
something you might like to know.
There are fairies everywhere: under
bushes, in the air, playing games just
like you play, singing through their
busy day. So listen, touch, and look
around—in the air and on the ground.
And if you watch all nature's things,
you might just see a fairy's wing.

—Author Unknown

Contents

Foreword

Living the Faery Life is an enchanting introduction to the magical world of the fae. Dr. Kac Young shares a wealth of knowledge and captivating insight into the supernatural realm.

Young begins by exploring the fascinating historical context of fairies. Timeless tales of these mystical beings span the globe from one continent to another. From the hills of Ireland to the rivers of Japan to the deserts of Egypt, fairy lore is rooted and deeply engrained within countless cultures throughout the ages. Legends of fairies are so much more than fanciful bedtime stories; they are powerful narratives that have shaped much of human history, and as Young teaches us throughout her book, they can still contribute to the richness of our lives today, if only we allow them to do so.

So how do we allow the fairies into our lives? How do we seek them out? What are the dos and don'ts? How do we create and maintain healthy reciprocal relations with these benevolent beings? Young graciously outlines the process for welcoming their presence into our lives, making magic accessible to everyone. She opens the door to infinite possibility and allows all who enter with pure intentions the opportunity to participate in this dance between worlds.

Genuinely connecting with fairies requires an authentic understanding of them, and Young's intimate familiarity with the fae grants her the authority with which to convey this understanding. She provides clear and practical guidelines for communing and connecting with the whimsical spirits on multidimensional levels, and this is an especially engaging addition to her book. She reveals that fairies exist on three geographical planes and describes the correlating characteristics and elements associated with each. The Upperworld, Middleworld, and Lowerworld serve as sacred and distinct dwellings for the fairies, who have unique preferences, pastimes, and personalities. With Young's guidance, we can learn to approach fairies appropriately and with clear purpose. Once we've entered this ethereal realm, is it really possible to return to a predictable mundane existence? One would think not.

Young further shares accounts of her own remarkable encounters with the "little folk." While many live according to the adage *I'll believe it when I see it,* Young emphasizes that some things must first be believed before they can be seen. The majority of our limitations are self-imposed, and the extent to which we can see depends largely on what we seek. Young's lighthearted, open-minded perspective has clearly opened her eyes to sights unseen by the common man. Her kindred connections and extraordinary experiences with playful pixies will leave readers with goosebumps and little doubt that there is more to reality than meets the eye. Young's insight is invaluable, and her reverence for the fae and their otherworldly kingdoms commands a deep respect and wholehearted affinity for their existence.

Young is a renowned and prolific author, and *Living the Faery Life* is yet another of her delightful masterpieces. Her passion and expertise shine through on every page, and this book is as much a gift as it is a guide. Rare is the work that prompts a paradigm shift for readers while moving them to reconsider their relationship to the natural world; this book does both.

No matter your prior perspective, by the time you've turned the last page, you'll be crafting fairy gardens, designing fairy doors, and welcoming wonders from otherworldly reaches.

In the words of Roald Dahl, "Those who don't believe in magic will never find it." Young inspires readers of every age to embrace the world of fairies and invite the magic of nature into their lives.

—ANAM CARA CAT
author of *How to Be a Fairy*
www.anamcaracat.com

Author's Preface

For many years, I lived in Los Angeles, in Hollywood to be exact. In 2006, I moved to Cambria, up the California coast just before you reach Big Sur. We had two acres surrounded by eighty-foot high pines and loaded with wildlife: wild turkey, families of deer, foxes, and bobcats, and hundreds of squirrels. It was a woodland paradise, and these animals were our friends. We had names for all of them, and we regularly gave them permissible treats and spoiled them rotten.

In 2016, I moved to Ventura just in time to be caught in the Thomas Fire. It ravaged our neighborhood and destroyed 90 percent of the houses around us. Our house was miraculously left standing with only a small amount of damage to the outside, the back fence, and some hillside landscaping.

We did not know if we had a house or not for three days. The news footage showed blazing structures, smoke, and destruction. I watched our neighbor's house burn to the ground on television. I figured our house would be gone, too. When I was finally allowed to return to the property, I discovered two major things; first, the damage at our place was small compared to the lots of smoldering embers surrounding our house. The inside was completely intact, and the garden area in the back, where I had placed a faery door, was unharmed. I attributed the saving of the inside to the bank of tall quartz tower crystals that I had on a cabinet in front of the window, and credited the protection of the backyard area to the faeries there, who often used the faery door I provided to make it easy for them to come and go.

There is no doubt in my mind or heart that we were protected. Do I believe in faeries? You bet your bottom dollar, I absolutely and unequivocally do. This book is my tribute to them and a love letter of gratitude to the magical beings who saved my house from the fires. For all they have done for me, I owe them this book, at least.

FAERY DOOR IN MY GARDEN THAT PROTECTED
THE GARDEN FROM FIRE, 2017.

THE UPPER HILLSIDE BURNED WITHOUT
THE PRESENCE OF THE FAERY DOOR.

Introduction

Many artists, poets, writers, musicians, and assorted other
human folk with creativity coursing through their veins
acknowledge that they owe their inspiration and drive to
muses who live in the faery world. Those invisible magicians
show their hands through the works of human artists because
they generously lend their inspiration and encouragement to
mortals who make faery magic visible in the mortal world.

In other words, when you look at a painting that transforms
you, hear music that inspires and uplifts you, or see a play that
opens your heart, it may well be the work of a faery.

How so? you ask. Because, for many faeries, it is their vocation
and sole purpose. Yet it can only happen to you if you are
accepted into the faery world. The faeries will decide if you are
worthy to be let in.

They live by a strong code. Faery ethics are not quite the same
as human values; rather, they value moments of high drama,
extreme passion, clear boundaries, and a set of core beliefs
shared by the entire faery community.

The world of faeries is a culture of stunning opposites. Where
there is joy, there are tears. Where there is laughter, there
is tragedy, and where there is fortune, there is dearth. The
very nature of a faery is capricious, elusive, sensitive, and
enormously powerful.

There are open doorways into the faery world, there are
pathways you should never cross without permission, there

is food and drink you should never accept, and there are souvenirs you should never take. If you are invited, enter at your own risk. When you enter the faery world, it is a deep, enchanting place full of humor, merriment, fantasy, and unbridled joy. Be wise, stay on the lookout for traps, and prepare to be asked to dance. Should you accept? Be assured there are consequences for everything in the faery world. Do you want to play?

Instructions for entry into the faery world lie within the pages of this book. Remember: Faeries cannot exist and will not stay in a place where no one believes in magic. Do you?

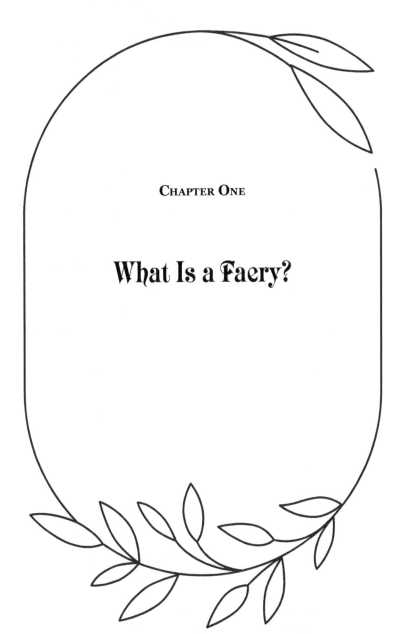

CHAPTER ONE

What Is a Faery?

Welcome to the world of faeries! The common terms *faery, fairy, fay,* or *fae* generally refer to the same thing: supernatural beings who live in natural places and possess magical abilities. There are those who would argue that *fairies* are the *good* beings and *faeries* are the evildoers. Like most things faery, the argument goes unanswered. Many discussions over centuries and endless cups of tea have concerned the manner and morals of these creatures. Are they real? Are they mythological, or are they simply products of fantasy created by the authors of fairy tales? What size are they, and do they have wings to fly? Are they green? Do they wear hats?

Those of us who have been touched by the writing of Sir James Barrie and the filmmaking of Walt Disney might think of faeries as beings like Tinkerbell from *Peter Pan,* (written in 1904) a twinkling little being with wings and a magic wand who lives on faery dust and sprinkles it wherever she goes. Was that your first introduction to faeries, or did you learn about them from books and bedtime stories? Were you able to conjure up your personal version of a faery, or did Hollywood directors paint your image for you?

For the majority of people in the Western world, Tinkerbell was our initial introduction to faeries. Films and television have had a giant impact on our imaginations, so much so that in fact, the IMDB website lists twenty-seven films as having faery content. (See Addendum A.) Somebody must believe in faeries for the studios to make that many motion pictures about them!

But where did these film subjects come from? The word *fairy* derives from the Latin word *fatum,* which when translated means *fate*. The word was also associated with the Greek Fates, three goddess sisters who spun the destinies of children at their birth and cut the threads of life. The other spelling of the word *faery* is derived from Old Gaelic, *fear sidhe*, which translates to *man of the fay* or *man of the mounds*. Now what, pray tell, does a faery have to do with mounds? A mound is the place underground and the location in history where faeries come to life and take form in European folklore and history. But before we bring our faery knowledge out of the Middle Ages and into modern times, let's have a gander at some other ancient folklore and how others may have conceptualized faeries in their own cultures.

Much like human history, stories about faeries are written by the victors. Faery tales and mythology are subject to the values and beliefs of the cultures that created them. They are rooted in the fears, morals, beliefs, religions, and handed-down lore of the society that created them. They may be real, or they may be fantasy; it all depends on how you look at them. For example, let's consider how creation myths differ culture to culture. Many myths and religions were fashioned because people feared death and sought to understand the world beyond. They sought explanations, and many origin stories were invented by people to answer the questions, "How did it all begin? How will it end? And how did that (magic) happen?"

Every culture known to humans has its own explanation for how we got here, who is in charge, and how we explain all the stuff that goes on, especially those elements that are seemingly magical. The answer reaches well beyond the question asked by the ever curious four-year-old, "Mommy, why is the sky blue?" Ancient people wanted to know how it all works just as we do, and, without ready answers, they created stories to explain it all based on who they were, what they believed, and how the "magic" showed up in their environment.

To answer the question of how it all began, the ancient Chinese myth of creation featured a creature named Pangu. At the beginning of time, there was nothing. This nothingness evolved into a primordial egg, which took 18,000 years. Within the egg, Yin and Yang became balanced energies. Pangu, a hairy giant with horns, emerged from the egg and began creating the world. After separating the earth from the sky with his axe, he held up the sky for another 18,000 years. As the earth grew thicker, Pangu grew taller. When he died, his breath became the wind, his left eye became the sun, and his right eye became the moon. That tale certainly explains how we got here.

Norse mythology as recounted in the Poetic and Prose Eddas describes creation as an empty world until the sons of Burr lifted the earth out of the sea. The Aesir created cosmic order by picking places for the sun, the moon, and the stars to live, thereby establishing the cycles of night and day. After that, a golden age resulted wherein the Aesir made tools and built temples. But along came three giant maidens who quelled the golden age. Undeterred, Aesir then created two dwarves named Motsognir and Durinn and, after an incident called "Dvergatal," man and woman were created. At that point, Yggdrasil, the world tree, becomes the focus of the story and the vehicle for explaining the world and cosmos.

The Mongols believed that when time began, there was only water. Udan the *lama* (holy person or priestly teacher) came down from the heavens grasping an iron rod. He stirred the water, which created wind, which then thickened and formed the earth. He began separating the earth from the heavens and dividing it into nine sections. He created nine rivers, and the first male and female, who were fashioned out of clay. They went on to multiply and became the mother and father of the world.

In Mesoamerica, it was believed that two Mayan gods called Kukulkán and Quetzalcoatl wanted to preserve their legacy by creating earth people who looked like them. They made three attempts: The first people were made of mud, but they fell apart. The second were made of wood, but they had no soul and fell out of favor. The third round of people were made from maize, the sacred food. It worked, and people were created to live on earth.

These are just a few creation myths that have been created by humans to explain their origins. Every culture has a story not only about creation, but also about the invisible world and the beings they cannot see, but to whom they attribute strange happenings, mischief, bad luck, misfortune, and mayhem. Why not? Somebody has to shoulder the blame, why not the unseen things? Why not faeries? Let's see how other societies describe them and define their magic.

What appears to be a common thread in historical research about faeries is that all cultures, old and new, seem to have considered them supernatural beings who are connected to the energies of the planet, nature, the stars, and the domains under the earth. There are several realms or dimensions where living creatures and supernatural beings exist that we mortals call "planes"; the cosmic plane, the earth plane, and the underworld plane are just three of many. Some faeries can move between the planes or can even manifest as humans, and they all appear to have some level of magical abilities, which may have been awarded to them in exchange for their lifetimes as nonhumans.

In Iceland, where the winters are long and the nights even longer without the sun, families gathered around fires to keep warm and tell stories. One such legend is that the first woman, Eve, we'll presume, went down to the river to bathe her children. Suddenly, she heard a booming voice, presumably God's, as the deity was paying an unexpected visit to the garden. She didn't have time to wash all of her children, so she hid the unwashed babies in the bushes, thinking she could fool God—oops. Of course God noticed and cast all of the unwashed kinder into the hills, rocks, and hidden places to dwell forever. They were named the *Huldufólk* and became the elves, faeries, trolls, and Hidden People of the region.

Icelanders are respectful of their (Huldufólk) faery dwelling places and never try to annoy them because the mischief of these invisible, supernatural creatures can wreak havoc on a human life. Stories tell of their stealing a baby and leaving a changeling in its place. Changelings are supernatural beings that are sickly, malformed, and patterned after monsters. They are frightening creatures to find, and it is even more frightening to discover that your infant has been switched with one of these. To preserve good relations with the Huldufólk, Icelanders craft small houses called álfhóls, or "elfhalls." These wooden houses are built especially for the Hidden People and are placed in cities as well as in the wilderness. They can be simple or elaborate in design and décor, and they are often accompanied by a small church in the hopes of converting the tiny ones. It has been said that 10 percent of the people of Iceland believe in these faeries, 10 percent do not, and the other 80 percent go along with the believers, just in case they are right. If you visit Iceland, you can make a game of seeing how many álfhóls you can spot. It is said that this is an ancient house-building tradition dating back centuries BCE.

Ancient Egypt and Samaria have writings that refer to other kinds of *beings* besides the gods and goddesses. To quote Donald A. Mackenzie in Chapter IV of *Demons, Fairies and Ghosts*, "All the world swarmed with spirits, which inhabited stones and trees, mountains and deserts, rivers and ocean, the air, the sky, the stars, and the sun and moon. The spirits controlled Nature: They brought light and darkness, sunshine and storm, summer and winter; they were manifested in the thunderstorm, the sandstorm, the glare of sunset, and the wraiths of mist rising from the steaming marshes. They controlled also the lives of men and women. The good spirits were the source of luck. The bad spirits caused misfortunes and were ever seeking to work evil against the Babylonians."

I have always wondered if the ancient Egyptians might have referred to the mystical spirits as "Phaories."

That certainly sets the scene for the historic conveyance of the belief in faeries via cultures that traded in merchandise and goods, as well as stories and traditions. What was believed in Babylonia BCE could easily have been carried by the tales of merchant traders to ports of call around the then known world, even into the frigid north like Scandinavia, where the faery sort were called Nornir, or Norns. These creatures, similar to the Greek Fates, were women who controlled the past, present, and

What Is a Faery?

future. They emanated from gods, elves, and dwarves and were considered to be the most powerful beings in the cosmos. They were mysterious in their origin and didn't appear to come from any other comparable beings in Norse lore. They appeared to be entities in a category unto themselves.

In Slavic lands, faeries were known as Vilas. These creatures became female when they surfaced on the earth and were born from nature and plants and easily transformed into wind, air, water, and fire. Symbolically, these faeries are attributed to either the underground realms or the top circles of the cosmos. They represent protection, control, nature spirits, and an assortment of *good* or *bad* characterizations including beneficence and mischief.

In the Vedic traditions of India, we see a mix of half-human, half-animal beings ranging from boars, to birds of all types, elephants, and even tigers. These supernatural beings are regarded as avatars of the gods and goddesses and perform certain vital functions in nature and life. For example, a snake called Naga controls and sets the weather. Budhi Pallien is the goddess of jungles, woods, and forests who rules and roams the land in the form of an agile tiger. I was particularly intrigued by the spirit being Homa Pakshi, who magically lays eggs which hatch in mid-air while she is flying across the sky. The offspring breaks free of the eggshell and learns to fly instantly, joining its parent in flight seconds before crashing to the earth. In Persian literature, this tale represents divine birth.

Sweden had the legend of the Tomte, a solitary and highly unsocial being thought to be half the size of a normal human, bearded, elderly, male, and is seen to wear farmer's clothing.

Despite being small in size, the Tomte possessed incredible strength. Wealth was attributed to his beneficence, which could disappear in an instant if he was disrespected, if he saw animals being mistreated, or if a person swore and used profanity. The Tomte was often believed to be the incarnation of an ancestor in his human's lineage and was considered to be one of the souls of the dead. If the Tomte was not left a bowl of porridge topped with a pat of butter, he might flee the farm and leave the owner in distress, with no possibility of good luck. The Tomte were both feared and honored, and they were placated, just in case.

While married to Hera, the Greek god Zeus had an affair with a nymph (faery) which produced his bastard son, Hermes. The Roman god Jupiter was raised by nymphs surrounded by animals in a cave. According to the legend, the nymphs were immortal beings. And, what about Pan, the very spirit of nature? He exists as a reminder that nature renews itself like a perpetual spring; like nature, Pan is also never-ending and immortally replenishing. He is a character with definite faery qualities and purpose.

We come now to the legend of the Sidhe, the Tuathe De Danaan, and the Shining Ones of Ireland, Scotland, Wales, Cornwall, Brittany, and the Isle of Man. Druids and bards passed down oral histories, and the legend has many variations but basically speaking, it went something like this.

Living in Ireland were a people known as the *Fir Bolg* who were descended from the *Muintir Nemid*, who apparently left Ireland to move to other parts of Europe, including Greece. However, some remained on the west coast of Ireland. The

Tuathe De Danaan, also descendants of the Nemid, grabbed the chance to conquer the land and subdue the Fir Bolg. They arrived from the northern cities of *Falias, Gorias, Murias*, and *Finias* in three hundred ships. The Tuathe brought with them many skills in science, building, architecture, and the arts, and they practiced magic regularly. They also communicated frequently with the dead via ceremonies, rituals, and special events. It was said they arrived in Eire in a cloud of mist and brought darkness across the sun for a few days. The darkness was more likely the blacked-out sun, which was blanketed in smoke due to the fact that they burned their own ships so they could not return home again.

The Tuathe Dé Danaan fought three battles while they ruled the green isle from 1450 to 1897 BCE. The first battle was against the remaining *Fir Bolg* on the west coast. It was known as *the First Battle of Magh Tuireadh*. The *Fir Bolg* were defeated, and the Tuathe ruled the island with a pantheon of gods, specifically including Danu, the goddess reflected in their name, "Danaan." Their second battle for control and rulership was *the Second Battle of Magh Tuireadh*, one waged against a people called the *Fomorians*. Alleged to be from the sea, they were monstrous beings with the heads of goats. Some historians attribute this battle to war against invading Vikings who sailed in large ships and bore metal helmets and colorful shields. Obviously they won, because they survived to fight a third battle with the *Milesians*, who invaded from the northern Iberian Peninsula and called themselves the *Goidelic Celts*. When the kings saw the invaders, they asked for a truce for three days. They asked the *Milesians* to anchor their ships nine waves from the shore. The *Milesians* complied. The Tuathe Dé Danaan used their magic to create a storm intended to overturn the ships and drown the invaders. Amergin, a clever *Milesian* poet, is said to have calmed the sea by reciting his verse over the waves. His people came quickly ashore at *Tailtiu* and conquered the Tuathe Dé Danaan. Since Amergin had worked the magic that allowed the *Milesians* to defeat their foes, he was asked to divide the land between the victorious *Milesians* and the conquered Tuathe De Danaan. He thought for a few moments and announced that all of the land above ground was to go to the *Goidelic Celts* while the underground would belong to the Tuathe De Danaan. They were led to the Sidhe mounds, where they disappeared underground to live for the rest of eternity.

The magical qualities of the invaders caught the Tuathe off guard and cost them their lands. Since then the Tuathe De Danaan, also known as the Shining Ones, dwell underground in the Lowerworld because of their magical gifts and abilities but can still interact with humans. The underground Tuathe De Danaan are associated with ancient passage tombs such as Brú na Bóinne, mounds, and all that is part of nature. These Shining Ones are the faeries that roam Ireland and have given us most of our faery lore.

Our modern views of faeries come from a plethora of Celtic literature and writings. The ancient Celts were spread over a large area of Europe stretching from Portugal to Russia and as far south as Southern Spain. Celtic artifacts have been found in the river Danube, which was named for the goddess Danu.

We owe most of our knowledge of the historical details to the Greeks and Romans who wrote about the Celts when they conquered their lands. After the victory of the *Goidelic Celts* at *Tailtiu*, the Celts in Europe became warriors for hire, as opposed to the Celts in Britain and Ireland, who were peace-loving farmers who practiced rituals connected to the earth. Like the Tuathe De Danaan, they lived by the cycles of nature: the lunations of the moon, the sequence of the sun, and the bounty of the earth, sea, wind, and cosmos. Cultural similarities have been noted in other countries as well. Persia had the Magi, the Babylonians had the Chaldeans, and the Celts had their Druids to advise them and lead their spiritual practice.

The number three was sacred to the Celts. They believed in three worlds: *Gwynvyd* (the Upperworld), *Abred* (the Middleworld), and *Annwn* (the Underworld). The Upperworld "Sky" was the domain of the Sky Gods and Goddesses and of Thunder Gods. Offerings were made by burning sacred fires so the smoke from the fires would reach the realm of the Sky. The Middleworld or "Land" supported the sacred realm of plants, trees, animals, stones, and humans. Stones and trees were especially cherished and venerated because, by its very existence, a stone was half in the underground and half above ground, thus having ties to both worlds, the Lower and Middle. A tree had its roots in the Underworld of Water, while its trunk, branches, and fruit lived in the Middleworld of Land and reached up as if to touch the Sky. Birds were revered as animals that could live on the land and fly up to reach the Sky.

The Underworld or "Sea" was the world of the ancestors of the *sidhe* or faeries. This below-the-radar world existed under the land but could be accessed through water sources like lakes, ponds, streams, and wells. It was a common practice to place offerings into bodies of water to honor the Underworld, the dwelling place of faeries. We will see later why stones, water, trees, plants, smoke, and feathers are ways through which we can contact the beings who dwell in the Underworld.

Magical, mysterious, and elusive, faery lore has been at the heart of stories and fantasies since the beginning of time. We have records of it in legends, books, and stories that have been handed down through the ages. Faeries bring meaning to the unexplained and give humans hope for goodness, blessings, adventure, and guidance. They are also the reflection of nature's signature, intelligent, skilled, self-perpetuating, in tune with the cosmos, and abundant. You can spot álfhóls in Sweden, and the Irish still build their cottages with the front and back door opposite each other so faeries can pass through at night. In the next chapter, we'll have a look at the different types of faeries and begin to decide who and what we want to believe in and why.

CHAPTER TWO

Who Are the Faeries?

Let's recall how we defined a faery in Chapter One: A *faery, fairy, fay* or *fae* is a legendary creature of mythical creation and folklore that is ascribed metaphysical, supernatural, or preternatural abilities. It is important to note that faeries have also been depicted as variously good or evil and full of blessings, curses, or mischief—all of which is likely true.

Throughout history, faeries have been defined as all of the above and more. And there is a myth attributed to each description. Faeries even made it into Shakespeare's plays in *A Midsummer Night's Dream*, which portrayed the warring faery king and queen, Oberon and Titania. To win the war and wear the crown of victory, Oberon enlists the help of Puck with his magical qualities and trickster nature. As characters in the play, faeries use their magical gifts to manipulate the human characters into behaving in abnormal ways, causing the mortals to end up in strange relationships and creating fresh rivalries. These faeries are more than sprinklers of faery dust, they are integral to the plot and outcome. Not to be slighted, Faery Queen Titania enlists her faery helpers too. Peaseblossom, Moth, Cobweb, and Mustardseed, come from the enchanted Green World of forests and meadows where ordinary reality as we know it is suspended and where anything can and does happen. In this magical setting, the audience is entertained in a dance of fun and enjoyment.

With the assistance of Walt Disney, the great civilizations that preceded us have, through their subjective lenses, defined who and what faeries are to them and how they believe the faery folk interact with humans. Here is a retrospective so we can see how the elusive beings known as faeries have evolved and expressed themselves through the ages.

Faeries in Multi-Cultural History

Africans believe the *Aziza* are beneficent faeries. They are alleged to have life spans ranging from 101 to 999 years. They are praised for their wisdom and intellect, and provide knowledge, guidance, and magical gifts to their human guardians. They have a deep connection to the earth.

In Asia, there are many faeries. The Chinese have the *Huli jing* and the *Mogwai*. The *Huli jing* are shape-shifters who bring both good and bad activities. They are recognized as fox faeries. *Mogwai* are evildoers and are categorized as monster-faeries.

The Japanese have the *kitsune*, who are fox faeries with the ability to transform into humans to blend in. There are thirteen different types of *kitsune*: Celestial, Spirit, Wild, River, Wind, Time, Sound, Forest, Mountain, Fire, Thunder, Ocean, and Void, each of whom has specific talents and perceptions. The Japanese also have the *Yōkai*, who are supernatural monsters with demon qualities.

Malaysians have the *pari-pari* (or *peri* in Turkey), who are motherly creatures that come to help and support humans with sincere hearts. They are famous for their beautiful appearance and benevolence.

In Persia, we find the *Peris*, who live in another world and are seeking paradise but must perform acts of penance before being allowed to gain entrance to paradise. They are mostly mischievous, which may account for why they have not yet attained their desired status.

In Vietnam, the *Tien* are known as angels, immortals, faeries, and otherworld spirits.

In Hindu and Buddhist mythology, there are the *Yaksha* who dwell in the woods and mountains; they are demons who haunt the wilderness and feast on travelers who wander through their territory—not nice faery folk at all.

In Ireland the *Aos Sí*, or *Aos Sidhe*, are the supernatural Shining Ones who were driven to the underworld and became faeries.

In Spain and Portugal, we find the *Duendes* or *Chaneque*, who are classified as paranormal beings similar to *Sprites* who bear a name that was shortened from the phrase *dueño de casa*, meaning possessor of the house. This classification also encompasses pixies and goblins. In Mexico, the *Chaneque* live in craggy, mountainous places as guardians and appear like toddlers with aged faces.

In Germany, they have *Elfen* or *elves*, who are named from the Norse word meaning "white being." Being multitalented, they are responsible for illnesses, magic, beauty, and seduction.

The *Encantado* from Portugal are spirit beings known as shape-shifting snakes or dolphins who live in an ideal underwater realm called *Encante*. They possess the magical ability to turn into humans.

The Greeks speak about *Nymphs*, who are female spirits from nature, with *Satyrs* as their complement.

In Welsh folklore and mythology, you will find the *Tylwyth Teg* or *Bendith y Mamau*, faery-like creatures that come from the otherworld.

In the principality of Asturias in Spain, you will encounter the *Xana*, a beautiful faery who lives in the forested areas near a pure body of water.

In Romania, you have the *Zână* (plural *Zâne*) who are positive creatures who dwell in the woods and perform benevolent acts.

The *Feufollet* are lighted faeries, spirits, or the ghosts of Cajun loved ones who come across the Louisiana bayou to visit in the form of a ball of fire.

The Mayans believed in the *Alux*, a small sprite-like creature; the Iroquois believed in *Jogah*, the small spirit folks.

Hawaiians believed in the *Menehune*, who were said to live in the hidden forests and island valleys, thriving on bananas and fish. They carried magic arrows to pierce the hearts of angry people and magically turn anger to love. They were rarely, if ever, seen by human eyes, but they were brilliant craftsmen and credited with overnight construction of mighty edifices. They were and are a busy lot.

In my research, I came across a wonderful website by Lady Arleta. She has collected and listed over 230 names and types of faeries. For further exploration of the faery world, I recommend Lady Arleta's site: ladyaleta.com/aleta/types.htm.

How do you explain disappearing objects or items that suddenly appear from thin air? What is the meaning of terrible things happening to you, or windfalls of positive blessings that come your way seemingly out of nowhere? Did something you just saw happen, or did someone or something cause you to imagine it? It's human nature to try to credit an original source or reason for everything, which is why practically every culture has a tradition of such faery beings. There can even be an inclination to view each blessing, or curse, as if it must have come from somewhere else Why not attribute these occurrences to a faery? To some, it makes logical sense to credit the faeries with either stirring up trouble or showering us with blessings. However, by so doing, we abandon personal responsibility and leave the realm of the mysterious entirely up to spirits and unseen forces. We then believe we are simply the victims or beneficiaries of their whimsy. Or we can formulate a personal set of beliefs based on our own spiritual power and create a strong relationship with the forces of the invisible world, which is what this book is all about.

Faeries have been called many things, as we have learned. You might already have a sense of what you believe faeries to be. Maybe you've even seen one or had a personal encounter with the workings of a faery. You've been exposed to opinions from historical sources and oral history, now you can decide what description works best for you.

Here's a Four-Step Process for Living with Faeries:

Step One: Define What a Faery Means to You (See below).
Step Two: Make Faeries Welcome in Your Home (Chapter 3).
Step Three: Get to Know the Faery Culture (Chapters 5, 6, 7).
Step Four: Connect with the Faeries (Chapter 8).

Step One: Choose your favorite definition (or make up your own): Faeries are:

- Ancient Celtic spirits of place
- Elementals, gnomes, and earth spirits who come up from the cracks and fissures in the earth
- Lesser deities in the Celtic pantheon
- Fallen angels
- Angels
- Foxes that can transform into humans
- Spirits of the dead or ghosts
- Astral or elemental spirits
- Sylphs, mermaids, sea nymphs
- Gaelic ancestors of the Irish and Scots who live in forests or mounds
- Tinkerbell

If you asked me what my definition of a true faery is, I would have to reach into my memory and say, *Helen*. Helen appeared as a tree squirrel that adopted me when I lived in a house in the forest in Cambria, CA. There were many tree squirrels who entertained us from behind the safety of our large picture windows; we watched their mating dances, their courtship rituals, and the presentation of their offspring. Underneath the oak trees, the deer roamed, poked around, and created families. Our acreage was alive with the natural world, and it was a joy to behold.

One day, a half-blind squirrel appeared on the back porch. She was persistent. She drank from the fountain, she peered in the windows, and she would not let us alone until we found some food for her. She was polite, patient, and grateful, if you can sense that quality in a squirrel. We named her Helen after Helen Keller, and we found something to set out for her to eat. Of course, we rummaged through the cupboards and found a special dish for her: we presented her with mixed nuts, healthy cookies, crackers, and pretzels. Helen indicated by picking them out of the mix that she loved peanuts, so on our next trip to the store, we had to buy a large bag of peanuts for Helen. Mind you, there were a lot of other squirrels in the forest, but Helen claimed us as her own.

We had conversations with Helen; she showed up every morning, stayed for most of the day, and said goodnight at dusk. Each evening, she made sure she caught our eye, flipped her bushy tail, and headed off into her tree.

HELEN KELLER SQUIRREL

One weekend, we had friends, Pamela and Ralph Ventura,
visiting us who were celebrating their twenty-fifth anniversary.
We had a little vow renewal ceremony for them and served
cake and champagne. Helen was there for all of it. She even
received a small piece of cake on her special dish because she
attended the party. Helen was always perched on the railing
in front of a window or visiting with one of our indoor cats
through the window. If we were late with her dinner, she would
thump on the kitchen glass to remind us. If we were going out
of town, we made sure to remind the pet sitter to include Helen
in the feeding schedule. We set out her bag of goodies with
instructions for feeding her.

One day, Helen got into the house. By then she was totally
blind, so I'm not sure she was really aware of where she was

headed, but I was sweeping out the sun porch and Helen walked right in, just like she was supposed to be there. I was frightened because I didn't know what she might do. I yelled out a frantic plea, "There's a squirrel in the house!" Then it dawned on me: This is Helen, and she is a friend. She'll be fine. Calm down. Welcome her, and she'll leave when the time to go is right. I sat down on the floor while Helen explored the room, found a crumb or two from off the rug, and headed back outside. I resisted the urge to keep her inside.

I had a deep connection to Helen. If I was having a bad day, stuck in some of my writing, or looking for an answer or a direction, I sought out Helen. Her little smile, her heart, and the sense of her presence transformed my dark feelings in an instant. She brought joy wherever she went. She followed us around from room to room, skittering outside on the porch and deck that wrapped around the house. Helen even showed that she missed us when we had been away for the day by pressing up against the window to make sure we were home safe.

After four years, Helen began to slow down a bit. We worried because there were bobcats and turkey vultures in the area. She wobbled up the back steps one day in a particularly slow fashion, and we were overcome with sadness. Helen seemed to be on her last legs. She stayed on the ground close to the windows all day. She could no longer leap and dash around. We fed her favorite foods to her, made sure she had fresh water, and fussed over her all day. That evening, she stayed a little bit later than usual. At twilight, Helen wandered away. She gave us her traditional evening goodbye and hobbled down the back stairs. We never saw Helen again. She had gone off into her netherworld, leaving us heartbroken but blessed. Many tears were shed and many sad days ensued until one day we came across a tree ornament of a silver squirrel. Years before we had shown the sparkling squirrel to Helen and she seemed to like it. To this day, that ornament sits in the kitchen window because it means that Helen, the faery squirrel, is still with us.

Before you start thinking that I've overreached, remember that faeries can transform into whatever shape suits their purpose in the moment. We were Helen's purpose, and she delighted us with her magic. She taught me to start looking for faeries in common places, to make little offerings, and to stand by for whatever magic might happen.

It would be self-serving to describe all of the magic she worked in my life, but there were plenty of times when Helen manifested opportunities and blessings out of thin air and sent them my way. I have no doubt in my mind that Helen is behind this book, among other things. She is a force in my life even to this day. I can't help but smile when I think of her.

If you asked me my essential definition of a faery, I would say that the faery realm is filled with a collection of beings, species and creatures that are connected to and rooted in specific places and governed by natural laws. They leave our world and the natural order of our reality when they wish and easily cross over into the spirit world, where they have access to unlimited knowledge, healing, and guidance. They are not limited to one physical form or function.

In either this life or a past incarnation, faeries became one with the purest energy and spirit of creation and now travel through the gates between the material and spiritual worlds, bringing ancient knowledge with them. They live in a reality where their souls are connected to what the ancients knew and we have forgotten. Their role is to bring that awareness back to us, and they will stay as long as it takes for us to believe. It may seem to us that they perform acts of magic, but the truth is we are all capable of magic and we are simply out of the practice of using our primordial gifts. Faeries can only exist where and when people believe in magic. What do you believe?

CHAPTER THREE

Making a Faery
Feel Welcome

In the last chapter, we learned about the different types of faeries that have existed in the creative minds of humans for millennia, in lore passed down through the ages. They seem to historically fall into one of two categories: Naughty or Nice. The truth about faeries is that you can believe what you want to. They are all made up! But you may know that already. Your believing in them makes them so. If you think this statement takes the magic and romance out of faeries, please reconsider. This, in fact, empowers both you and the faeries.

If believing in faeries makes them so, then what do you want to believe? That they are the positive benefactors of humanity or the evil-bringers of mischief and bad fortune? It's up to you. The further truth is that the faery kingdom does exist. What you think and how you project your belief to them determines how they manifest themselves to you and behave toward you. Step One asked you to define what a faery is in your mind.

This new concept of Faeryland gives you total freedom to think as you choose and thereby bring what you want into your life. You do not have to be limited by someone else's concept that faeries are ill-tempered, bearded, evil people who bring sadness, mayhem, and chaos, even grief, into your life. Nor should you worry that faeries will be flying over your head sprinkling faery dust that messes up your mind and your carpet. Faeries are what you want them to be. They have certain rules, characteristics, and qualities, and you can draw on those, but you are unlimited in your possibilities with them.

Let me tell you about my first faery encounter. It was in Hollywood in 1972, and I was living in a duplex on a side street just above Franklin Avenue. I had been living in Paris for a year studying with and working for French and English theater directors. I was thrilled to come back home after eleven months of both exciting and hair-raising adventures. My roommate's mother, a lovely woman, came to visit, and she brought over a pair of little apple dolls that she had purchased at a fair. She thought they were cute and would look nice in our new apartment. The dolls were dressed up like a country grandma and grandpa sitting in small handmade rockers. My first reaction was that they were creepy because they were originally apples, hand-carved and shrunken to a small head, then dressed up with hand-sewn clothes and plastic hands. We put them in our dining room on the buffet by the window. In time, I got used to them and began to appreciate the detailed handiwork. In a few months, I was even saying hello to them when I entered the room.

I did my work at a typewriter on the dining room table across from the dolls. I was working late one evening, I looked into the living room and saw an apparition; it was translucent, smoky, and surrounded by a thin aura of blue light. I didn't know what I was seeing, but I was a little bit spooked. My roommate was working late and didn't get home until after eight o'clock. When I told her about what I had seen, she asked if I'd been drinking wine, and I told her, "No, I was working, here," gesturing to the dining room table.

The apparition came again the next night. I was beginning to think the apartment was haunted. A friend of mine told me that the University of California at Irvine had a department of parapsychology that studied such encounters. I called them and made an appointment. They came to my apartment and asked me a ton of questions. Fortunately, my roommate was around, and as she heard my description and saw their reactions, she began to think I was less crazy.

The expert consensus was that my apparition was a *poltergeist* spirit roaming the house. It was capable of making loud noises, knocking things over, and moving objects around. They informed me that the spirit was harmless and I should try to engage in a conversation with it the next time it appeared. I was secretly hoping they would take whatever-it-was with them and leave me to my work and my peace of mind. They didn't, but at least I had an explanation, and they asked me to keep a record of the visits and occurrences. "Wow," I thought, "Now I'm taking notes for a ghost." The people from UC Irvine were very nice. I felt a lot better after their visit—certainly a lot better than I'd felt after the visit of the ghost.

As life went on, I lost my fear of the otherworldly visitor. The poltergeist made itself at home. From time to time, I would see its form in different rooms. I left a few cookies out for it one evening. They were gone in the morning. Okay, spooky! My relationship with the poltergeist was on-again, off-again for about a year.

When it came time to move to a new apartment, my roommate said I could have one of the apple dolls. I didn't actually want either of them, but I didn't want to hurt her mother's feelings, so I took grandma. In my new place, which was about ten blocks away from the old duplex, the apple doll again sat in the dining room on her rocker as I worked at the big wooden table, just as I had in the previous apartment. My roommate took the grandpa doll.

A few weeks after the move, when we were living in different apartments, I took care of her dog while she went away for an overnight. When she came to pick him up, she brought me the grandpa apple doll. "He's lonely for his wife," she said as she handed him to me. I placed him next to grandma, and it wasn't three nights before I saw the poltergeist again. What was going on? I placed another call to the parapsychology department at UC Irvine.

Before they returned my call, I had another unsettling incident. One night while I was working at my desk/dining room table, I heard what sounded to me like machine-gun fire. I immediately hit the floor and crawled under the table. The sound kept coming, but it wasn't until I smelled popcorn that I realized there was popcorn popping on the stove. What? I lived alone now, so who was in my house popping corn on my stove? I crept into the kitchen tentatively, and on the stove, I saw one of those all-in-one magic popcorn poppers that comes complete with the pan and corn included. All you have to do is rip off the cardboard lid, put it over a fire, and the popcorn expands and puffs right up into the foil balloon. (If I remember correctly, it was called Jiffy Pop.) There was no one in sight. I turned off the stove and cased the place. Nothing.

The person from UC Irvine called back the next day. They said it was highly unusual for a poltergeist to move with a person to another location. They asked me to keep records and said they would check back in a month. "Yeah," I thought, "If I'm still around." I went back to my work, nibbling on the popcorn the poltergeist had cooked for me the night before. One morning a few days later, I was already almost late for work, nearly out the door, but I couldn't find my shoe. I needed my work shoes to be able to stand on the cement studio floor all day during the taping of the television series I was working on. I could find one shoe, but the other was nowhere around. I was so frustrated, and I looked everywhere in the small, one-bedroom apartment. I finally had to find a different pair of shoes; they were not as comfortable, but I was out of time. Our shooting days were long. My feet hurt after twelve hours standing on concrete floors. I got home after nine o'clock and found my lost shoe neatly placed on top of my pile of papers on the dining room table. What the…? I made notes of this for the college professors.

The next thing that happened was probably the most bizarre. I had bought a nice pair of diamond stud earrings as a little gift for myself. They were my pride and joy. I took excellent care of them, cleaned them often, and made sure they were safe every night when I took them off. One morning, I couldn't find them in their little container. I looked everywhere for three days and feared that someone had stolen them. I was heartsick: no earrings. But the next time I opened up a four-roll package of toilet paper (a sealed package with no opening), I discovered my diamond stud earrings in the bottom of the package inside a toilet roll core. Yep, plain as day: I had found my beloved earrings. My emotions were running between feeling thrilled at the discovery and terrified of what was going on in my house. I was sitting at the dining room table when the apple dolls caught my eye.

I arose from the table in slow motion and walked over to the dolls, "Are you the ones doing this?" I asked—I swear they both smiled. Holy criminy! This was unbelievable. I called the parapsychology department and left a message explaining what was happening. When they called me back, they asked me, did I believe in faeries? I said, "Kind of, why?" They said these kinds of activities sounded more like faeries than poltergeists. I went back to the apple dolls and asked them point blank, "Are you faeries?" I swear they grimaced and lowered their eyes.

All this time I had been dealing with faeries and hadn't known it. It changed the entire game. I called a meeting. I sat down at the dining room table, brought out the items they had been involved with and announced. "Okay, this has been fun, but it's over. You may not touch any of my work, my business records, my money, my jewelry, or anything else of value to me or my well-being. Do you understand?" The place was still. "Furthermore, you've had your fun and we're done with mischief, understand? No more games, no more hide-and-seek, no more stealing, and please, stop frightening me! What do you want? Leave me a list. But no more pranks!" You could hear a pin drop. I looked at the apple dolls and softly said, "That means you, too." That time, I'm quite sure I saw them smile.

I told a good friend about this and she howled. After she stopped laughing, she said, "Leave gifts out for them. They love presents." What a great idea! I started doing that right away. I left them bits of food, pieces of candy, sparkly toy rings, buttons, ribbons, and whatever I could find. I thought it might be rude to leave them apple slices, so I left orange pieces instead. They became particularly fond of those gummy candied orange slices coated with sugar. Those and gum drops were the hands-down favorites.

Once I had identified the source, I was no longer frightened. I didn't stay awake all night fearing someone was sneaking into my house. I felt like I had invited guests in my home. This was my first, and quite dramatic, introduction to faeries.

Since then, I have made a place for faeries in my life. I love them, and I train them to live in harmony with me. They are welcome to be anywhere they want to be, but they cannot do naughty things. They mess with me every now and then and hide things, but it's always dumb things like my keys, my favorite pen, or my rhinestone reading glasses, and I always find them. They do, however, help with bigger things. I told you the story of the fire in the Author's Preface. The faeries around me are productive and helpful, and I praise them and play with them. They have flowers to smell, a garden in which to frolic, and treats to sustain their whimsy. I leave little toys, balls, and shiny rocks, and I made a rock faery circle for them to dance in; oh, and chopsticks. They seem to love to play with chopsticks.

Step Two: Make faeries feel welcome. Arrange objects for their amusement, create a play land, leave out treats, and respect the areas you have designated for them. As you read through this book, you will learn what they like and how to best welcome them into your home.

The trick with faeries is to write your own myth. Place faery things around and invite them in. Make sure you play by their code of ethics (coming up in the next chapter) and leave them special treats. Be very clear that you attract to you the type of faeries you believe in and desire to meet. Never yell at them, but remember that they respond to firmness and frankness—as they did for me. Believe me, I didn't know what I was doing back then, but I can see that, like little children, they enjoy boundaries and feel loved because you care enough to set them.

You can read the faery code of ethics in Chapter 5, and then learn the best ways to connect with them in Chapter 6. I break faeries down into three sections or worlds: the Upper, Middle, and Lower worlds. They come in all shapes and varieties, and you can summon the ones you want to interact with, not on command, but by invitation and giving them a good *fáilte* or welcome.

CHAPTER FOUR

Where Faeries Live

After years of research and reading, I have come to the conclusion that the Japanese and the Norse interpretations of faeries are the most accurate. As mentioned in Chapter 2, the Japanese believed in thirteen different types of faeries: Celestial, Spirit, Wild, River, Wind, Time, Sound, Forest, Mountain, Fire, Thunder, Ocean and Void. The Nordic people believed in the three wells and nine worlds of Yggdrasil, the world tree. I think the concept of having three worlds associated with the elements of life is the right path when we consider where faeries exist and find their homes. There are certain places where faeries feel the most aligned and comfortable.

Step Three: Getting to Know the Faery Culture.

Faeries exist on three geographical levels: the Upperworld, the Middleworld, and the Lowerworld. Each world is connected to one or more elements and embodies certain characteristics. I have grouped the faeries we have discussed so far and arranged them according to the world they most often inhabit. If you are a student of faeries, you may find some of your favorites missing. Feel free to include them in the listing that follows. These are not hard and fast rules, simply ideas for organizing the different types of faeries.

The faeries for each of the three worlds are imbued with different personalities and assignments that fit their level. It's like a department store: housewares on one floor, cosmetics on another, and luggage in the basement. The spiritual view of the three faery worlds harkens back to the Norse mythological tree Yggdrasil and the spaces of existence to which it is connected.

The Upperworld (Gwynvyd or Sky) connects with the element Air. This is the realm of inspiration, muses, creativity, higher thoughts, guiding principles, ideals, purposes, kindness, faith, belief, promises, psychic connection, intuition, and forgiveness. This is the world we long to live in and strive to align with. You may want to think of it as faery heaven, complete with winged beings. These faeries most likely play harps.

The faeries associated with the Upperworld are those who live in the air, survive on the wind, and make merry in the breezes. They are bringers of blessings and can be also be manipulators of fate. They come from a world of power over the visible world and are not afraid to use their magic for good, or if necessary, to teach life lessons. Associated with this world are the Vilas, Norns, the Shining Ones, Aziza, Tien, Duendes, Fates, Sylphs, Windsingers, and Sprites.

The Middleworld (Abred) is connected to two elements, Earth and Fire. The faeries of this realm are workers, accomplishers, helpers, makers of things, builders, manifesters, caretakers of all things natural, guardians of the forests and animals, nurturers, restorers, sailors, and gatherers of gold. Think of them as the cobbler's helpers in the old children's tale.

The faeries associated with the Middleworld are: Elves, Kitsune, Yaksha, Sidhe, Changelings, Huli jing, Zâne, Menehune, Tomte, Mogwai, Alux, Nymphs, Pari-pari, Jogah, Brownies, Puca, Phooka, Goblins, the Fetch, and Pixies.

The Lowerworld (Annwn) is associated with the element of water and is also called the Underworld. It is the world of transformation, purification, renewal, rebirth, change, transmutation, death, penitence, the collective unconscious, core beliefs, sexuality, initiation, and psychic communication. In this world, we can change our lives for the better when we plunge into the watery depths and explore ourselves. Here we can make the decision to reemerge renewed and reborn, ready for a fresh start.

The faeries associated with this realm are: Trolls, Hidden People, Encantado, Selkies, the Tylwyth Teg, Water Sprites, Sirens, Merrows, Kelpies, Mermaids and Mermen, and Sea Wight.

Below is a chart for easier reference.

World	Faeries
Upper (Gwynvyd) Air	Vilas, Norns, Shining Ones, Aziza, Tien, Duendes, Fates, Sylphs, Windsingers, Sprites.
Middle (Abred) Earth and Fire	Elves, Kitsune, Yaksha, Sidhe, Changelings, Huli jing, Zâne, Menehune, Tomte, Mogwai, Alux, Nymphs, Paripari, Jogah, Brownies, Puca, Phooka, Goblins, the Fetch, and Pixies.
Lower (Annwn) Water	Trolls, Hidden People, Encantado, Selkies, *Tylwyth Teg*, Water Sprites, Sirens, Merrows, Kelpies, Mermaids and Mermen, and the Sea Wight.

The three worlds can of course be expanded to include additional faeries. This is just a starter list. If you have favorites, you can easily identify the qualities they embody and place them into the correct world. This will be helpful for Chapter 6, which is on Connecting with Faeries, where you will find three separate ceremonies designed to connect with the faeries of the different worlds. When you find the world and the faeries you are drawn to, use the rituals and make the connection. The faeries will become your greatest helpers, allies, and friends. In the next chapter, we will learn the rules of conduct by which the faeries live.

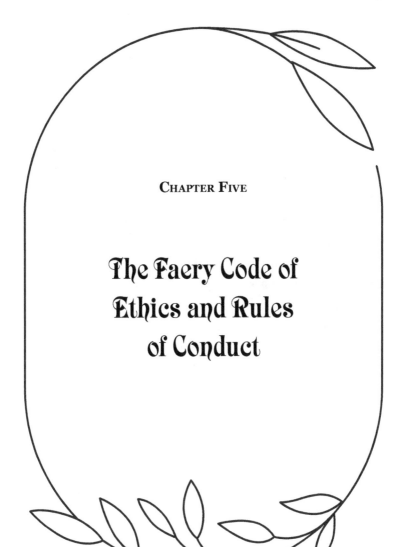

CHAPTER FIVE

The Faery Code of Ethics and Rules of Conduct

Within the books and websites I have researched about faeries over the years, some of the so-called *rules* for interacting with them make me laugh. In this book I would like to challenge and reframe some of the claims about how to best interface with faeries.

First of all, it's true that they are a very different race. Remember, they are stuck back in time with regard to their evolution. They have the mindset, manners, and social mores of a race from 1500 BCE. That's when they were conquered and forced into the hills and underground. This leaves them with very different ideas about how to interact with the world. When you watch a television series based in a different time period, you are watching the characters think, act, and speak as they might have more than a century ago. It was a very different time, and it is entertaining to see how they thought, reacted, and lived their lives back then. With that in mind, we can have a new look at some old fears about faeries and put them into a fresh perspective.

Old Rule of Engagement	Newer Consideration
Faeries are easily offended.	Yes, this is true. They are sensitive and didn't grow up with modern brashness and confrontation. They think and speak in flowery thoughts and words, so getting right to the point and the bottom line does not fare well. Take your time. Speak to them with delicacy and care. Always be super polite. It's old-fashioned, but speak delicately and consider their feelings first and foremost.
Never say *Thank You* directly. This acknowledges that you are in debt to them.	If you thank a faery, they will feel they gave you something and you owe them in return. They are extremely reciprocal-minded and believe when a gift is given, it implies a debt is created in return. What you do instead is appreciate what they have done for you or what they have given to you. (See below for details.)
Never lie to a faery.	Correct. Faeries have special sight and magical insights, and they can see the dark layers of a lie and it infuriates them. They will react negatively to an untruth.
Never take food or drink from a faery.	Correct. They come from the earth. Their food and drink do not have our modern standards of purity. They may make a tasty drink from foxglove blossoms that could kill you. They do not mean you harm, but their ways of making food and drink could be fatal to you. They love making preparations of hallucinogenic materials, which is fine for their magical selves but might send you into a coma.

The Faery Code of Ethics and Rules of Conduct

Never accept a gift from a faery.	You have to decide individually. They are reciprocal by nature and will expect something in return. They also may ask for a gift that you cannot provide, so it's a good idea to walk away in case there is a hidden meaning in the gift. You'll know what to do after working with the faeries for a while.
Do not make a contract with the faeries.	Here's another odd fact. Faeries interpret language differently. They are clever and may twist a meaning. You can do this, but only with extreme caution. Be sure you understand what you are agreeing to in *faery* terms.
Never mention a newborn. Faeries are fond of children and may take yours, leaving a changeling in exchange.	Perhaps when people lived in the woods and left their children alone while they worked in the fields this was a concern, but nowadays, it's only remotely possible a faery would steal your child. However, err on the cautious side.
Never announce your dealings with faeries.	Correct. Faeries are very private. If they have bestowed blessings on you, keep it private. (See below for more details.)
Never give faeries your real name. They will have power over you.	In the past, your name meant everything about you: your family, your birthplace, and your ranking. Today, that is not the case. However, play with the faeries. Make up a name just for them and you accomplish two goals: making them special and keeping your privacy if you feel you need to.

Never say *I'm sorry* to a faery. This means you are indebted to them.	Once again, you'll be the judge, case by case. (See below for further instructions.)
Don't invade their privacy.	Correct. Do not disturb their garden, except to clean it from debris, and don't peer into their world unless invited.
Don't dance with faeries. They will trap you.	Faery music and faery dance are ritualistic and could mesmerize you. The chance of anything evil happening is slim to none, but you have to judge for yourself. (See below for thoughts and good advice on this.)
Always keep your promises to faeries.	Correct, to faeries and everyone else. They'll know if you skirt the issue.
Faery debts will always be repaid.	You may not know when or where, but faeries will always repay your gifts, offerings, kindnesses, and the gifts of the garden you provide for them.
Gifts from faeries are tricks.	They might be, but they are usually well-meaning and fun-loving tricks. Faeries like to play. They love to laugh, and they may be playing a trick on you to make you laugh, too. They also like to spread joy, and this may be their attempt to get you to lighten up. You'll know. Always give them the benefit of the doubt. You can always ask them, politely, what their intention was. That usually clears up any mystery.

The Faery Code of Ethics and Rules of Conduct

Iron is harmful.	Correct. Iron is deadly to faeries, even when contained as a mineral in the stones you leave in the garden. Clear their space of all iron implements to keep them healthy.
Always be polite.	Faeries come from gentler times. There was no verbal abuse, cussing, or character assassination. They were gentle before they were banished and remain so. Harsh words, scolding, cursing, and yelling wound them deeply and may even scare them away.
Never date a faery.	History has told us that faeries and human have paired up in the past. I think anything is possible, but you will have to be well-versed in the faery milieu in order to make this work. It's more than learning a new language, it's stepping way back in time mentally and emotionally.
Faeries don't believe in God.	Faeries believe in the highest world of nature and magic. They are connected to the primordial forces of creation—chaos, order, karma, and intelligence.
Faeries are mean tricksters.	Faeries love to play. They can't discern the difference between tilting the picture on your wall and dumping a pitcher of blackberry juice on your white carpet. They always opt for the laugh and the giggle. What may seem like a trick to you is most likely innocent faery entertainment.
Faeries are greedy.	Never. They abhor greed. Faeries love to share.

Faeries love to laugh.	Yes. They love it when you laugh with them all the time.
Faeries love to love.	Yes. Faeries are the essence of love itself. They love to love, express love, and be loved in return.
Faeries need your help.	Faeries want you to help them care for nature, animals, plants, and all living things.
Faeries are competitive.	Faeries enjoy excelling and playing hard. They enjoy a good challenge, fairly played and honestly won.
Faeries are loyal.	Yes, but trust and loyalty have to be earned. They are wary of strangers, but once befriended, a faery will be your friend for life.
Faeries are curious sorts.	Yes, they are inquisitive. They like to know how things work, what they taste, feel, smell, and sound like. They like to poke and prod objects and learn everything they can about the magnificence of nature.
Never dig in faery areas.	Yes. Leave their special places alone. If you disturb them, they will seek a payback.
One morsel of a pomegranate seed given to a human will render them unable to leave the underground.	Yes, this is very possible if given to you by a faery. Graciously refrain from indulging.

The Faery Code of Ethics and Rules of Conduct

Faeries will test a human to discover their code of behavior.	Indeed. Before faeries befriend you, they want to know your beliefs, values, and practices.
Respect is the most important thing to a faery.	Yes. This is a race of being who have been maligned and mistreated by their foe. Being respected is as important to them as breath.
Never sing a faery song.	Faeries are protective of their music. Sing your own tune, not one of theirs, unless they specifically invite you, and be cautious.
Faeries love nature most of all.	Faeries are deeply connected to everything in nature. They are personally hurt when they see nature mistreated. They will do anything to fix, heal, and celebrate everything in the natural world. They are enchanted by the sound of a raindrop and the sight of a budding rose.
Faeries are easily displeased.	Absolutely. Faeries rely on truth, honesty, kindness, and respect. If they are disrespected or neglected, they may remind you of their displeasure by creating a mess.
Ask permission before you take something or change it.	Yes. Faeries respect natural order. If you are going to change something in the environment, ask for permission. Even if you pick a flower, ask permission to do so.
Ask a faery three times for a request.	Yes. The number three is the faery magical number. It is the number of creation and carries a high vibration.

A rainbow is a faery bestowing luck.	Yes. When you see a rainbow, you will know faeries are at work doing good.
Do faeries speak a special language?	Their first language is Fey, and their second language is Tacital, which is not spoken but expressed through music, art, dance, magic, and body language. Faeries can read both the body and emotional language of all beings.
Do faeries go to school?	Faeries are taught hunting, swimming, gathering, foraging, dancing, playing music, climbing, sewing, and magic.
Do faeries have holidays?	Yes, faeries celebrate Beltane, Midsummer Night's Eve, Samhain, and Midwinter or Yule.

The Faery Code of Ethics and Rules of Conduct

Below are some more details concerning the statements above:

One: Never say *Thank You* directly. This admits that you are in debt to them.

As we said, faeries think differently. They think in quid pro quo terms. What you do instead of saying *thank you* is to marvel, flatter, and appreciate the gift. "What a beautiful _____." "This is an amazing _____." "How thoughtful of you to bring me such a lovely _____." "I've never seen anything as magnificent as this." "What a generous thing to do." This makes the faery feel like they have done something special, which they have, and it displays a creative side to how you value the item or deed and its significance to you.

Two: Never announce your dealings with faeries.

Faeries are very private as we mentioned. They are not boastful, they are humble and self-effacing, and this is why they respond to praise and accolades. They can't say it about themselves but vibrate with good juju when someone else says flattering things about them. Again, we are talking about the faery mindset here. As an example, I sought faery approval before writing this book because I recount stories and encounters with the faery world. I was honest with them when I said I wanted to tell my stories about the faeries I knew and clear up some of the misstatements that abound. They had a faery council meeting and let me know I could write it with their blessings. What I discovered later, and this must have caused them great guffaws and giggles in-house, is that they probably brought me the offer in the first place. It was not a book I had outlined and pitched; it was a book that was offered to me to write, out of the blue. Of course the faeries wanted me to write it! I laughed when I thought about how long it took me to figure that out.

Three: Never say *I'm sorry* to a faery. This means you are indebted to them.

If you inadvertently insult a faery or hurt their feelings, you'll know it. They will do something to let you know they are unhappy. If you find some things rearranged, tipped over, upended, or broken, that's because a faery feels wronged in some way. If you say, *I'm sorry*, you are admitting guilt and intention. We don't think that way, but faeries do. We think we are being accountable for a mistake and apologizing for it. They see it as you intentionally hurting them, which you and I know you did not. It was probably just a simple mistake or an oversight. What you do instead to avoid the linguistic issues is to say something like, "I understand you are upset. Is there anything I can do to make you feel better?" "You are my friend, and I am unhappy when you are unhappy. How can we make it better?" "I have brought you (these treats, these gifts) to make you happy." "Your happiness is very important to me. Let's sing a song together." They will respond to these efforts. No debt is implied or assumed, and the mood will shift in a positive direction. Are you seeing the subtleties?

Four: Don't dance with faeries. They will trap you.

This is a perfect example of revisionist history. Perhaps a gentleman or a lady disappeared for a while and eventually came back home. It was easier to tell the family that they had been absconded with by faeries then they had run off with a lover for a tryst. Or, they had too much to drink, fell into a hole, and blamed it on the faeries. I think it may have been convenient to use faeries as an excuse for their own misdeeds. That's my opinion. Now, it's true the faeries crave dancing. They can dance wildly, they can get out of control as in the ecstatic dances of the mystics, but, all in all, they are experiencing a euphoric high when dancing and do not want to entrap anyone. I like to think of some of their goings-on as more like raves from modern times. They probably get all charged up on foxglove blossom juice or consume some hallucinogenic mushroom soup and dance their little feet off. In order to stave off all fear of engaging with faeries, my thought would be to not drink and only mildly engage in dance. Watch your step, but enjoy the celebration. Leave when you think anything is getting past your comfort zone, and remember faeries will expect payback if anything goes wrong according to their way of thinking. This way, you can make your own decisions and dance with faeries or not depending on your instincts and intuition. Remember, eat nothing and drink nothing faeries offer you. Be polite, but turn down the temptation to indulge.

Five: Do faeries have holidays?

Yes, they have four major holidays. **Beltane** (May Day) runs from sunset on April 30 to sundown on May 1. **Midsummer's Night** is celebrated in June, the night before the Summer Solstice, which falls between June 19 and June 25 and includes the preceding evening. **Samhain** or All Hallows' Eve runs from sunset October 31 to sunset November 1. **Midwinter** (Yule) is celebrated between Dec 21 and 24 on the eve of the Winter Solstice from sundown to sunset of the next day.

The bottom line is that we need to remove any fears we have about faeries. They are supernatural beings, and they will reciprocate to us whatever we put forth to them. If we operate out of deceit and underhandedness, that's what we will receive from the faery kingdom. If we operate from a spirit of love, honesty, fairness and generosity, that's what will be returned to us. All of the hocus-pocus and fear around their magic and negative spells can be handled by being accountable for what you project.

The faeries' code of behavior and ethics differs from those of modern humans, but it doesn't take too much effort to realign our thinking and support their values if we want to connect with them and share a beautiful friendship. It's up to us to bring out their best side and positive qualities. We also have the power to rile them and stir their dark side, but who in their right mind wants to incite faery wrath? It's better for everyone when we take the affirmative path, join the parade, and take a walk in their tiny shoes as if we were a faery, too.

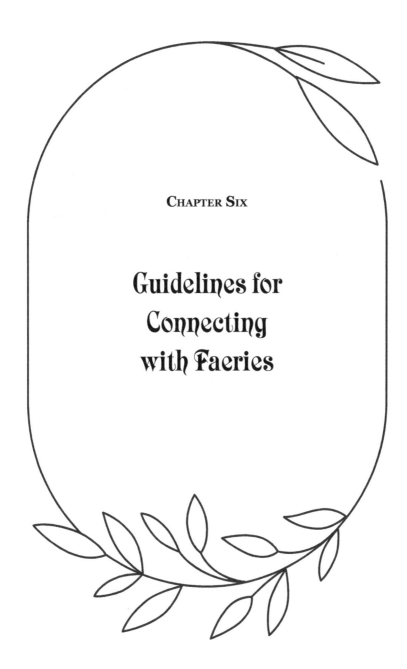

CHAPTER SIX

Guidelines for Connecting with Faeries

tep Four: Learn the rules for connecting to faeries; in this chapter and in Chapter 7, you will learn the methods and rituals for reaching out to them.

The realm of faeries is a sacred place filled with magic and infused with a bounty of beauty from the natural world. Faeries may slip in and out of our world at whim, when summoned, or when something needs to be made right. But make no mistake, entering the faery consciousness is no easy feat for a human. It takes willingness, practice, patience, and humility. The faeries don't need us; we need them, or we may simply want to connect with them and make friends in another dimension. If we have been called to connect with entities and energies from the otherworld, we need to begin adjusting to them, their vibration, and their ways of looking at life.

There are nine requirements for contacting a faery.

1. Pure in Heart
2. Clear of Mind
3. Love of Nature
4. Respect for All Living Things
5. Appreciate Music
6. Joy of the Dance
7. Affinity for Whimsy
8. Proclivity for Laughter
9. Believe in Magic

Being *Pure in Heart* is the first prerequisite for contacting faeries. It means that you must have good intentions; that you only desire good to come from your contact with faeries, you wish no ill or evil on anyone or anything, and you will only use this connection for the betterment of humankind and all other beings. If you are pure of heart, you will not ask for anything malevolent or deceitful from faery magic and you will not harm any living creature with your intentions or requests. If you want to get even with someone or pay them back for something they did to you, look elsewhere. Do not use faery magic for revenge or to settle a score. Make sure your request is in alignment with each of the nine categories and that it is based in goodness, kindness, and a desire for only positive outcomes. Only then should you proceed with contacting the faery world.

This first precept may require you to forgive others and let go of negative thoughts and intentions. You may need to pray, release, and clear your heart of resentment or hate before attempting this connection. Because faeries live to help, they don't want any part of settling human scores. Faeries are skilled at telling fakes from the truth, so when you want to step into the faery world, make sure you are pure of heart. Put a lot of love in your heart and move to point two.

Clear of Mind is the second point. Be clear about your real reason for wanting to have faeries in your life. If you are just looking for faery magic to help you, don't take the next step. Faery connections need to be reciprocal, and the faeries you contact must see that there is benefit on both sides. They will determine if you are a good candidate for their love, affection, kindness, generosity, and magic. If they suspect you have evil or selfish intentions, they will steer clear of you like a fetid swamp. Be sure you want to give back to them as much as you take. Think of interacting with the faery world like a scale:

There can't be an imbalance. It won't fly. That's why we must give as much as we ask. If you are Pure in Heart and Clear of Mind with your intention and your sense of fair exchange, you can move to point three.

Faeries have an insatiable love of and connection to all things natural. They *are* nature. They see themselves as trees, plants, moving water, and twinkling stars, and they experience their reality as air, earth, water, and fire. They can transform into any of the elements at any time and *become* the elements of creation. Faeries don't stir up a storm; they become the wind and dance wildly. They don't command the waters to be still; they transform themselves *into* water and calm themselves from within. They can do this because they deeply love and understand all the elements of nature, and, in that spirit of love and unity, they can actually embody the elements. This quote, attributed to Gandhi, encapsulates the definition of faery magic: *Be the change you want to see in the world.* This sentence is written in harmony with the spirit of faery philosophy and describes how and why they change themselves in order to make a change in the world.

Hand in hand with Love of Nature is Respect for All Living Things. To connect with the faeries, we must feel respect for everyone and everything around us. This means we have to respect everyone, even if we don't agree with them. We respect others because they are alive and they are part of the world, and because we need to learn to understand them. It does not mean we have to like them or agree with them. We just need to respect them as beings, whether human or animal, animate or inanimate. They have a right to be here, to breathe the same air, feed from the bounty of the earth, and stand under the same sun and moon as we do. They have the same rights as we do to prosper, enjoy life, make love, and create a life for themselves. We have to let them be and support them in their right to be different. The place we draw the line in the sand is if they come to harm us or prevent us from exercising the same rights. Even in the faery world, these are known as inalienable rights: the right to life and the pursuit of happiness. These rights cannot be taken or given away. They belong to everyone and everything on the planet, every person, every animal, every rock, tree, plant, and flower, even broccoli. If you can practice and perfect the meaning of this phrase, Respect for All Living Things, in your everyday actions, you will change your life forever.

For many people, this is a lifelong quest. It removes generational hatred, the need to be right, dominance, bullying, racism, sexism, and any other "ism" that blocks equality for everyone. It elevates the gift of being alive and the universal right to live your own life according to the principles of unity and equality. Faeries want us to arrive at this awareness because it mirrors their own and brings peace of mind and peace on earth.

Next in line in the prerequisites for connecting with faeries is the Appreciation of Music. Music is at the heart of our universe. Every note is connected to nature and the cosmos. Many notes played together form the chords of existence that bind our worlds together. Music is like the tree Yggdrasil; it reaches into all three worlds and blends all levels of life into one living entity. We must educate ourselves to appreciate all types of music. The faeries relate to tunes and tones that harmonize, are not too fast, and represent the kind and gentle ear of the universe. I would say faery music is lyrical and lithe at its core.

The music of our universe can be heard in the drumbeats of the tribes in Africa, in the bells of ancient China, the Yemenite Shofar horns of the Middle East, and the conch music of Hawaiian shamans. Taken together, they represent the music of generations of cultures and traditions. When you listen with your heart and soul, you arrive at a true appreciation of the purpose of music, which is to transport you to a sacred place.

You must have music to dance! Next on our list is the Joy of the Dance. It doesn't matter if you have classical ballet training or two left feet. Dance is essential to faery life. Dance moves the body and is like an internal massage for all of the organs that keep us alive. Faeries know this. They know that dancing keeps life energy moving through us. Dancing connects you to other beings when you join in with a sense of joy and celebration. When dancing, the heart is happy and overflowing with thoughts and emotions.

The act of dancing awakens your inner child, frees you from burdens, brings light into dark places, and increases the pheromones of happiness and harmony within the body. When you dance, you activate the spirit of the universe and give it expression. The faeries dance to strengthen their bonds to each other in the Lowerworld and to affirm life. They give way to the moment and let it be all that exists in that snippet of time. While they are dancing, life abounds, spirits soar, and they prove that all is well and full of what is good. Next time you dance, let your purpose be to open your heart to the vast well of joy that lives inside. Abandon your cares and step into the moment of freedom and release that is the gift of the dance. Realize you are in sacred service to the faery world and that through your dancing you will heal strife and mistrust. And here you thought dancing was just about moving your hips. In the faery world, it is so much more than just a shake, shake, shake of your booty.

Faeries live to dance and dance to live. They know how important it is to engage in dancing and celebrating the spirit within. Some faeries start their morning with free-form dance. Some dance because they are watching the sun rise. Some dance when it sets, and others dance in the moonlight. No matter how and where you like to dance and express your spirit, put it in your agenda and never ever put it off or forget to dance. There is an opportunity to dance in every moment you are alive. Look for the moments and put them to use. You'll have a lot to share with the faeries when they come to meet you. They'll probably want to dance! Be sure you leave room in your garden for dancing.

Next on our prerequisite list is an Affinity for Whimsy. This means you have to know how to play. You need to foster your sense of humor and find delight in even the most mundane things. The faeries do! Faery laughter is heard in the trees, coming from the mounds and echoing across the hillsides. When you connect to the faery world, you might walk by a garden and hear a rock laughing. Say what? It really isn't a rock; maybe it is a faery disguised as a rock. Who's to say for sure? Faeries can transfigure into different forms with the snap of a finger, so you will never know exactly where or what the laughter is coming from. It's faery laughter and could be anything, anywhere.

Faeries delight in playfulness and the spirit of fun and mostly delight in the wonders of nature. They will laugh uproariously when a daisy tickles their nose or when they blow the seeds off a dandelion to tell the time of day. Faeries don't need watches; they tell time by how many breaths it takes them to blow the seeds off the flower. They also make dandelion wine and use the stems to decorate their houses: whimsy at work.

Faeries love things that sparkle; they love ribbons that dance in the wind, and they adore bubbles, sweet smells, pungent aromas, and warm pudding. Faeries love children because they are free in their hearts and giggle and smile at the same whimsical things that faeries do. If you have forgotten whimsy, spend a few hours with a baby and watch how they gurgle, giggle, and coo. It will awaken your inner center of whimsy and put the smile back on your face. Smiles of whimsy come from inside, they are not painted on or forced. They come from deep inside and bubble up to the surface just like a baby's giggle.

Whimsy and joy are partners in this prerequisite. Whimsy begets joy, and joy begets whimsy. It's a reciprocal partnership which results in giggles and appreciation for the silly bits of life. Babies often giggle and laugh when they fall down. After they giggle, they get up and try again. It's all part of the game. So the next time you want to capture a little of your inner faery, engage in whimsy. Let go with a giggle that comes from the delight center in your belly, and let it emerge across your face like a ray of sunlight. Then go ahead and let that light shine. Let it lead to playfulness, and bingo! You're in a state of whimsy. Whimsy wakes up a faery better than an alarm clock. Look around and see if you can spot one. Invite them into your circle of whimsy, but watch out for the stampede. You may incite a riot of faeries anxious to join into your moment of joy.

The Proclivity for Laughter follows on the heels of an Affinity for Whimsy. It begs you to consider the humor in all things. Even the most serious moments of life can be a source of humor. Comics make a living out of turning their stories of pain, humiliation, anguish, and life lessons into comedic jests we can all enjoy. How many times have you laughed at a comic who told you about something dreadful in their childhood that is uproariously funny now? The faery rule is to laugh with, not at, someone or something. To laugh at or ridicule is to break the Respect for All Living Things rule. Faeries don't do that. If someone drops a plate of dishes, it might be a source of amusement, but faeries wait a beat to make sure the person isn't hurt. Then they laugh. And they might even applaud to make light of a situation that was an accident. Faeries never make fun of anyone or anything, unless the fun is being made by the person or thing and the laughter has been invited in. Faeries are very fair that way. They will go out of their way to find amusement in their surroundings. They might engage in some mischief to create a situation that merits laughter. In general, their intentions are not malicious; we will get into the subject of mischievous-seeming faeries in a later chapter.

A two-pronged carrot makes the faeries laugh; dolphins jumping out of the water make them laugh. Finding a cricket sitting on a toadstool brings forth a guffaw. Coming across a pinecone that has been devoured by a hungry squirrel is a cause for gales of giggles. Encountering a lopsided bucket is the source of many snickers. Humankind may not find these particularly funny, but in the faery world, they are hilarious.

The point of this prerequisite for humans seeking faeries is to learn to find the little delights in life. It encourages you to observe and watch for small enchantments that surround you. It suggests you pay more attention to what is going on around you, look for humor and fun in life, and allow yourself to be enchanted by what you see. What delights you? A kitten playing with a ball of string? A puppy trying to walk for the first time? A squirrel trying endlessly to climb up a pole, and then sliding back down again as he seeks the contents of your bird feeder? Is there an elderly person on your block who has stories to tell that tickle your fancy? Can you laugh at the birthday cake you put in the oven that exploded, leaving souvenirs all over the inside of your oven? Or the sunflower seeds you planted too close together that took over your yard?

The trick with this prerequisite is to discover the humor in the moment. If you can laugh at little disasters, you will discover the humor of the faeries.

Our last guideline is to Believe in Magic. We're not talking about stage magic of the kind you see on talent competitions. We're talking about real magic, possibilities, probabilities, and supernatural acts. To connect with faeries, you have to be willing to be astonished, to be amazed, to let your jaw drop in awe at a miracle. You have to be willing to be breathless, to sit on the edge of your seat in expectation and release a squeal of joy when it happens. You have to believe not only that something can happen, but that it will. The faeries do. Magic is a common denominator in their day-to-day lives. Performing magic is as easy as sneezing to a faery. They have learned how to move between the realms, the worlds, and manage the energies to make things happen. To them it's not magic at all, just a universal talent they learned as kids and use at whim.

Faeries don't take their ability to do magic for granted. They still hide their gold and cover their plants in the frost, but they do know how to transform and reassemble matter into a new shape and form. Here's the real secret; they can teach humans to work with magic, but they'll only do that after they have tested you, known you for some time, and come to the decision that you measure up and are qualified to learn their skills. Faeries can live for a thousand years. They have plenty of time. They are on the lookout for beings they trust to pass their knowledge along to. Are you the one they are looking for?

You now know how to become a worthy ally to the fay realm by keeping these principles in mind. Now it's up to you to become someone the faeries want to befriend and love. Oh my, and if they cherish you, well, then you're in for good. Read the list every day. Practice each rule and engage in faery antics, and you may soon find yourself dancing around stone faery rings with fresh flowers in your hair and a truly magical touch.

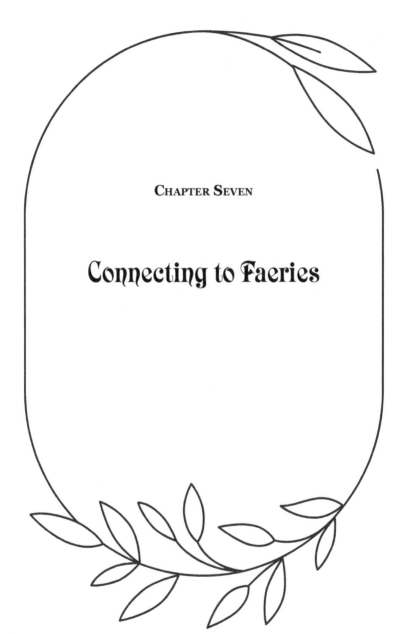

CHAPTER SEVEN

Connecting to Faeries

In Chapter One, we learned that the old-world Celts believed in three worlds: *Gwynvyd* (the Upperworld), *Abred* (the Middleworld), and *Annwn* (the Underworld). Three was their sacred number, and multiples of three is what we will honor here to connect with the faeries. We will use, three, six, nine, and twelve to make our connections.

Faeries who live in the Upperworld (Gwynvyd, or Sky and Air) respond to smoke, birds, and treetops. Faeries who live in the Middleworld (Abred, or Earth and Fire) respond also to trees, animals, plants, stones, and humans. Humans can connect with Faeries of all three worlds on the Middleworld level. Trees, plants, and stones have connections to the Middleworld as well as the Lowerworld because they have roots that reach underground. The Lowerworld (Annwn or the Underworld, the realm of Water) is the world of the seas, minerals, ponds, streams, and wells.

In Norse mythology and the lands where the original Sidhe came from, the image of the tree Yggdrasil was a simple yet powerful way to explain and to conceptually connect the heavens, the earth, and the underworld.

Like the Celts, the Norse people believed in this linear linkage, but they defined it according to nine levels. The Celts kept it simpler with their Upper, Middle, and Lower worlds, and so shall we.

Faeries with wings are typically attributed to the Upperworld (the realm Sky and Air). But not all faeries have to have wings. Wings may have been totally invented by filmmakers and art directors. I always like to consider the question: If all faeries had wings, how could they maneuver into their mounds, hillsides, underbrush, and forests? Wings would definitely catch on the underbrush. I prefer to believe that these magical beings would simply manifest wings if and when they needed them. Faeries are, after all, practical beings.

Faeries in charge of the Upperworld (Gwynvyd, or the Sky or Air) might be the Sylphs and the Windsingers. They do not seem to age and are talented shape-shifters. They have been known to assume a human form and typically live in high places and on mountaintops. These faeries are kind and helpful. They wish the best for you and help you to see things clearly. They are sources of inspiration and mental agility. You might seek their friendship if you need to see the big picture, get out of a rut, develop a broader perspective, find your creative expression, and tone your mind to be quick and nimble. How could these qualities enhance your life or give you insight into a situation?

Faeries in the Middleworld (Abred, or Earth and Fire) might be: Brownies, Puca (Phooka), Pixies, Goblins, Elves, or even the Fetch. These are the practical faeries. They keep your life level and functioning on the right path. Although some might say that they can be mischievous, you might need the help of a Brownie if you are overwhelmed with chores and have a long to-do list as they are efficient in the home. (The Brownies girls' scouting group got their name from these faeries in 1925.)

The Puca keep you on your toes. They can act as guardians or can bring you a comeuppance if you get careless or lazy. You would seek the Puca if you needed a metaphoric arm around your shoulder or a monitor of your deeds. The Pixie is childlike, mischievous, and totally harmless. If you need some levity or fun in your life, ask the Pixie. Pixies remind us that we have to play or we become rigid, stuck in our ways, and grow old before our time. The Pixie will always show you the way to put some innocence and joy back into your life. Goblins are the opposite of Pixies. They have malevolent tendencies. They are jealous, greedy, self-centered, and magical. They can steal from humans and are not to be trusted. It is unlikely you would even want to contact a Goblin, but knowing they are there is good to know and fair warning.

Elves are the great leveler. They can be helpful to you, but if they feel mistreated, they may harm something close to you as a payback. Elves are wonderful as long as you are fair and honest with them and appreciate their efforts. Finally, we have the Fetch. This faery is unique. It will give its life to warn you of impending death. This could be mortal death or the death of your old ways. It will sacrifice itself to give you a heads-up. The question is whether you will listen or not. Each Fetch has but one life to give, and it sincerely hopes you won't waste it.

Faeries from the Lowerworld (Annwn or the Underworld, the realm of Water) might be: Sirens, Merrows (or mermaids), Kelpies, the Sea Wight, or Selkies. The Sirens are temptations and those things that lead us down the wrong path. They may seem harmless, but they are ruin wrapped up as a present. The Merrow are mermaids and mermen. They represent something that isn't as it seems. It can swim, mesmerize, and taunt, but it is a sea creature and cannot live on land. It cannot keep its promises of love, and if you are not watching what you are doing, you can crash your ship onto the rocks. You would seek help from the Merrow faeries if you need to understand what is going on beneath a disguise. If you are looking for truth, the Merrow can take you there. The Kelpies are shape-shifting beings usually seen as horse spirits of the water. You would contact them when you want to move on, to radically change from one situation to another, or to leave the past behind. The Kelpies are radical instruments of change. When you want to change course or find a different way, they are the spirits you contact for help in accomplishing that. The Sea Wight is the queen of the watery underworld. She oversees all of the activities of the faery world and she controls the weather. She is a quiet creature who does not seek recognition but manages the power of the weather; she rules over life and death, floods and famine, verdant life or scorched earth. When you want to work the earth or take a sea voyage or need the help of the elements in some form, the Sea Wight is the one you would seek and humbly approach for help.

The Selkie is a creature of transformation; traditionally a she, a Selkie can also be a male. A Selkie lives in the sea, but if they contact a human and want to live as one, they can come ashore, shed their skins, and take on a fully human form. They are gentle creatures, nurturing and simple, and if crossed, they will return to the sea. You would seek the help of the Selkie faery if you wanted to make a shift in your life, shed the past, and move on to a different life, one simpler and truer to your original nature.

Who or what you contact depends on what you seek, what kind of faery help or inspiration you need, and how you want or are willing to go about contacting the faery realm.

Methods and Rituals for Making Contact with Faeries

The Upperworld

The Element of the Upperworld is Air or Sky. Air rules
the mind, inspiration, ideas, angels, clarity, wisdom,
knowledge, spiritual teachers, muses, psychic powers, higher
consciousness, memory, intuition, the celestial realm, and
spirits and ancestors. The emotion of Air is Joy. The time of day
it governs is Dawn. The best times to contact faeries are dawn,
dusk, noon, and midnight. The places you can find them are
by the sea, on the shore of a lake, in the woods, on ley lines, on
specific fairy paths, under a tree, or in a beautiful garden. (See
Chapter 8 for how you can make a faery garden.)

To reach the Upperworld faeries and connect to and honor
them, you might perform a ritual using smoke, incense,
feathers, bells, crystals, music, essential oils, and natural
plants. If you like to smudge, you can choose from these herbs
and easily make your own smudge sticks. The faery qualities of
each of these herbal attractors are listed below:

Plant	Faery Qualities
Cedar Sage, *Salvia roemeriana*	Generous, bestowing of favors, moral and good
White Sage, *Salvia apiana*	Cleansing, purifying, transforming
Lavender, *Lavandula*	Insight, psychic connection, happiness, healing, tranquility
Mugwort, *Artemisia vulgaris*	Dream enhancer, inspiration in sleep time
Rosemary, *Salvia rosmarinus*	Cleansing, balancing, forgiving, purifying
Palo Santo, *Bursera graveolens*	Connection to the Divine, physical healing, holy
Yarrow, *Achillea millefolium*	Protection, love, universal healing, sacred

If you make these herbs into smudge sticks, be sure to let them dry well before use, or, alternatively, you can place dried herbs in a bowl and burn them. It would be an excellent idea to invest in an abalone shell to use for your smoke and smudging rituals. You should consider finding or purchasing a large feather, perhaps from a turkey, a raven, or any nonprotected bird you choose. The feather is your instrument to send the smoke skyward as you say your prayer or incantation so it will reach the faery realm you are seeking. Discovering your feather should be a journey unto itself. If you would like to incorporate colored feathers, below is a chart that explains which color attracts what virtues. Feathers speak loudly to faeries as they find them enchanting and irresistible. You can arrange the colored feathers representing the qualities you seek during the ceremony, and the faeries will tune right into the meaning and help you manifest them.

Feather Color	Quality
Black	Protection
White	Purification, Hope
White & Black	Transformation, Change
Red	Courage, Good Fortune
Blue	Psychic Awareness
Green	Healing
Yellow	Mental Clarity, Joy
Pink	Love, Honor, Virtue
Purple	Universal Connection to Spirit
Gray	Peace
Brown	Patience, Timing, Remaining in Place
Spotted	Release and Forgive

Place a stone and a small bowl or cup of water out for the faeries. Prepare some honey or jam, an apple slice, some berries, and a cracker or small pile of cereal bits along with a mirror. You may want to bring a compass if you want to ask questions of the faeries.

The emotion is peace and the time of day is dawn.

The crystals and stones would be:

Apophyllite, Prenhite Clear Quartz, Herkimer diamond, Amethyst, Celestite, Peridot, or Pink Calcite.

The essential oils would be:

Lavender, Lemongrass, Melissa, and/or Peppermint.

Ceremony to connect with Faeries in the Upperworld:

1. Set your stage in the woods, by the sea or a lake, or in a garden.

2. Prepare your offerings: in a small bowl, berries, fruit, cracker, cereal, and a dab of honey or jam.

3. Gather your crystal stones, bells or chime, smudge stick, music source, essential oil diffuser (I use a portable plastic battery operated one for outside), and white candle. Arrange everything to the right of the candle.

YOUR FAERY ALTAR AND OFFERINGS

4. Ring your bell. Turn on your diffuser. Play your music. Open the ceremony. Read your opening prayer—either in your own words, or:

My invocation is my invitation. My intention is goodness. My belief is in magic and the faeries living in the Upper, Middle, and Lower worlds. My heart welcomes this sacred meeting.

5. Light your white candle; dedicate it to the radiant bright energy of love and light, purification, and the realm of the faeries:

I light this candle to illume the passageway between two worlds, the world of the seen and the unseen. I invite in the good spirits, the faeries of the Upperworld and all of my guides and helpers. Let us engage together in love, friendship, and communication. May the veils lift, our hearts open, and the way be cleared for our exchange. Welcome all.

6. Name the stones you have brought and speak the qualities they represent. Place your stones on the mirror and say:

Today I present the crystals and stones of: _____

They represent the qualities of: _____

7. Place the feathers you choose, listing each quality that they represent.

The feathers I present represent the qualities of _____, which I hope will bless us all.

8. Light your smudge stick and fan the smoke skywards. You may wish to ask a question or proffer a request to the Upperworld faeries at this time. Burn your herb bundle until smoke is produced. Your answer will come in the form of which direction the smoke blows. If the smoke

rises upwards in the center, the question is clear. If it blows toward the north, you have the answer in your own wisdom. If it blows south, you can expect change and transformation. If it blows east, you are clear of this situation. If it blows to the west, you will need to do more inner work and release blocks before the issue can be resolved.

9. Say a prayer of your own making or use the one below to address the faeries:

    I come before you to honor you, to seek your friendship, and to ask for your help. I believe in you. I love you and I respect you. This sacred smoke is a tribute to you, your magic, and your gifts. Today, I seek your friendship and your help for (name your issue or request). I offer you this tribute as a symbol of my sincerity. I open my heart and my life to your magic and generosity.

10. Spend as much time as you wish. Engage with the faery energy from your heart. Ask them how they are doing and if they need anything. Share your feelings with them. Make it an exchange between friends.

11. When you have finished, thank them for their willingness to come into this realm.

12. Close the ceremony with gratitude and leave them with a blessing.

    Thank you for the time you have spent with me. I appreciate your willingness to come into my world for a time. I am grateful for your kindness, and I value all that you have done and can do for me. I reciprocate with gifts and good feelings. I bless all of you with beauty, humor, joy, and laughter, and I wish all of you long and happy lives.

Leave the biodegradable offerings behind for them. Pack up your bells, stones, diffuser, and supplies and return to the Middleworld transformed and at peace from having been in the aura of faery spirit.

The Middleworld (Abred, or Earth and Fire)

The elements of the Middleworld are Earth and Fire. Earth rules grounding, strength, nature, success, stability, foundation, fertility, death, rebirth, animals, and wisdom. The element of fire rules passion, power, strength, transformation, joy, energy, fuel, lust, destruction, work, and action. The emotion for this rite is Love, and the time of day is Noon.

A faery in the Middleworld might be a Brownie, Puca (Phooka), Pixie, Elf, Goblin, or even the Fetch. If you want to connect to the faeries of the Middleworld, they will respond to trees, animals, plants, stones, fires, and humans. Collect your items as you did for the Upperworld Air ceremony. You will need music, a white candle, crystals, essential oils, a small drum, a small burner for resin or frankincense (see instructions following the essential oils list just below), feathers if you choose, and your food offerings.

The crystals or stones for the Middleworld are:

Earth: Jasper, Carnelian, Shungite, Black Tourmaline, Agate, Green Jade, Preseli Bluestone, or Petrified Wood.

Fire: Ruby, Garnet, Sardonyx, Sunstone, Amber, Fire Agate, or Red Tourmaline.

The essential oils are:

Earth: Cypress, Vetiver, and Patchouli.

Fire: Basil, Clove, Cedarwood, Frankincense, Juniper, Nutmeg, and Orange.

To burn resins such as frankincense, you will need a charcoal disc, a lighter, tongs, a nugget or two of frankincense resin, a handful of sand or pea-sized gravel, and a fire-safe incense burner made of metal or pottery. Place the sand or pea gravel in the incense burner. Holding the charcoal disc in your tongs, light it for ten to fifteen seconds until it ignites. It will begin to show tiny sparks when it is lit. Put the charcoal in the incense burner and leave it for a few moments until it is covered in a thin layer of gray ash. Place the nuggets of frankincense on the hot disk with your tongs. The fragrant frankincense will begin to smoke and create an uplifting and enchanting scent for your ceremony.

Ceremony to connect with Faeries in the Middleworld (Abred, or Earth & Fire):

1. Set your stage in the woods, by the sea or a lake, or in a garden. Prepare your offerings in a small bowl: berries and other fruit, cracker, cereal, and a dab of honey or jam.

2. Gather your crystal stones, small drum, incense and resin burner, music source, essential oil diffuser (I use a portable plastic battery operated one for outside), and a white candle. Arrange them to the right of the candle.

3. Turn on your diffuser. Sound your drum. Play your music. Open the ceremony. Read your opening prayer— either in your own words or:

My invocation is my invitation. My intention is goodness. My belief is in magic and the faeries living in the Upper, Middle, and Lower worlds. My heart welcomes this sacred meeting.

4. Light your white candle, dedicate it to the radiant bright energy of love and light, purification, and the realm of the faeries:

   I light this candle to illume the passageway between two worlds, the world of the seen and the unseen. I invite in the good spirits, the faeries of the Middleworld and all of my guides and helpers. Let us engage together in love, friendship, and communication. May the veils lift, our hearts open, and the way be cleared for our exchange. Welcome all.

5. Name the stones you have brought and list the qualities they represent. Place your stones on the mirror, saying:

   Today I present the crystals and stones of: _____
   They represent the qualities of: _____

6. Place your feathers you choose, mentioning each quality that they represent.

   The feathers I present represent the qualities of _____, which I hope will bless us all.

7. Light your incense burner and the resin nugget.

8. Say a prayer or use the one below to address the faeries:

   I come before you to honor you, to seek your friendship, and ask for your help. I believe in you. I love you, and I respect you. This sacred smoke is a tribute to you, your magic, and your gifts. Today, I seek your friendship and your help for (name your issue or request). I offer you this tribute as a symbol of my sincerity. I open my heart and my life to your magic and generosity.

9. Spend as much time as you wish. Engage with the faery energy from your heart. Ask them how they are doing. Inquire of them if they need anything, listening for any responsive impressions. Share your feelings with them. Make it an exchange between friends.

10. When you have finished, thank them for their willingness to come into this realm.

11. Close the ceremony with gratitude and drumming, and leave them with a blessing.

    Thank you for the time you have spent with me. I appreciate your willingness to come into my world for a time. I am grateful for your kindness, and I value all that you have done and can do for me. I reciprocate with gifts and good feelings. I bless all of you with beauty, humor, joy, and laughter, and I wish all of you long and happy lives.

    Leave the biodegradable offerings behind for them. Pack up your stones, drum, feathers, diffuser, and supplies, and return to your Middleworld transformed and at peace from having been in the aura of faery spirits.

The Lowerworld (Annwn or Underworld, Water)

The element of the Lowerworld is water. It rules emotion, intuition, love, feelings, the unconscious, healing, forgiveness, transformation, lunar power and tides, fertility, and self-reflection. This world represents the archetypal mother, an energy which like water creates new life as it nourishes the earth, the sea, and animal life.

The emotion is Compassion. The time of day is Dusk.

Choose crystals for this ritual from these:

Fluorite, Lapis Lazuli, Chrysocolla, Aquamarine, Apatite, Turquoise, or Lepidolite.

The essential oils for this rite are:

Blue Chamomile, Eucalyptus, Jasmine, Myrrh, Sandalwood, or Bergamot.

The water element promotes love, healing, peace, compassion, reconciliation, forgiveness, friendship, nurturing, tranquility, deep sleep, dreams, psychic abilities, and self-purification.

Faeries from the Lowerworld (Annwn or the Underworld, Water) might be Sirens, Merrows (mermaids) Kelpies, the Sea Wight, or Selkies. If you want to connect to the faeries of the Lowerworld, they will respond to shells, water, sand, mirrors, and minerals. Collect your items as you did for the Upperworld and Middleworld ceremonies: you will need music, a white candle, crystals, essential oils, a container of sand, some shells, a small mirror, a small wooden flute, a blue cup or glass of water, feathers if you choose, and your food offerings.

Ceremony to connect with Faeries in the Lowerworld (Annwn or the Underworld, Water):

1. Set your stage in the woods, by the sea or a lake, or in a garden. Use a small mirror as a centerpiece.

2. Prepare your offerings: in a small bowl, arrange berries, fruit, crackers, cereal, and a dab of honey or jam.

3. Gather your crystal stones, bowl or glass of water, sand, shell, music source, essential oil diffuser (I use a portable plastic battery operated one for outside), and white candle. Arrange them to the right of the candle.

4. Make a sound with the small flute. Turn on your diffuser. Play your music. Open the ceremony. Read your opening prayer—either in your own words, or:

My invocation is my invitation. My intention is goodness. My belief is in magic and the faeries living in the Upper, Middle, and Lower worlds. My heart welcomes this sacred meeting.

5. Light your white candle, dedicate it to the radiant bright energy of love and light, purification, and the realm of the faeries.

I light this candle to illume the passageway between two worlds, the world of the seen and the unseen. I invite in the good spirits, the faeries of the Lowerworld and all of my guides and helpers. Let us engage together in love, friendship, and communication. May the veils lift, our hearts open, and the way be cleared for our exchange. Welcome all.

6. Name the stones you have brought and mention the qualities they each symbolize. Place your stones on the mirror, saying:

Today I present the crystals and stones of_____ .
They represent the qualities of_____ .

7. Place the feathers you choose, listing each quality that they represent.

The feathers I present represent the qualities of _____, which I hope will bless us all.

8. Pour your sand into the container and place the shell on top, saying:

Sand from the earth and sea. My tribute to water.

9. Say a prayer of your own devising, or else use the one below to address the faeries:

I come before you to honor you, to seek your friendship, and to ask for your help. I believe in you. I love you, and I respect you. This sacred water is a tribute to you, your magic, and your gifts. Today, I seek your friendship and your help for (name your issue or request). I offer you this tribute as a symbol of my sincerity. I open my heart and my life to your magic and generosity.

10. Spend as much time as you wish. Engage with the faery energy from your heart. Ask them how they are doing. Inquire of them if they need anything. Share your feelings with them. Make it an exchange between friends.

11. When you have finished, thank them for their willingness to come into this realm.

12. Close the ceremony with gratitude and drumming, and leave them with a blessing.

    Thank you for the time you have spent with me. I appreciate your willingness to come into my world for a time. I am grateful for your kindness, and I value all that you have done and can do for me. I reciprocate with gifts and good feelings. I bless all of you with beauty, humor, joy, and laughter, and I wish all of you long and happy lives.

    Leave the biodegradable offerings behind for them. Pack up your flute, stones, diffuser, mirror, and supplies, and return to your Middleworld transformed and at peace from having been in the aura of faery spirits.

Each of these rituals for the three worlds involves different items to honor the realm in question. In truth, you don't need any props; you can contact the faery world without adornments. But as we learned in connection to the faery code of ethics and principles, they adore ceremony and ritual. They will delight at your efforts and your gifts to them, and you will attract in the faery world the measure of what you give out. I like to err on the side of generosity. It has never failed me.

Become familiar with the three worlds. Understand the difference, and seek out the faeries of whatever realm fits your needs. You will know intuitively which kingdom can help you. The faeries do not operate like we do. They have their own motivations and desires. Get to know them before venturing into their world, and you will be surprised at how receptive they can be.

When we choose to live with faeries and their energy, our job is to supply an opening for them so they can find us and share their faery energy and light. Here is a ceremony you can do to show the faeries they are welcome in your home.

Officially Welcoming the Faeries

The very first thing you want to do is create some kind of an altar or magical circle or space that is dedicated to the faeries. Even the corner of a room is fine. Select a nice piece of cloth that is colorful, handmade or otherwise special. Or create a faery garden indoors or out, depending on where you live, and select some flowers and herbs from the garden to grace your altar. In your faery garden, make sure there is a faery door, a place to place offerings, and maybe a small wishing well, tiny furniture, shining rocks, sparkly things, and a stone circle for dancing around.

Use a scent, essential oil, or natural smudge stick to create an aroma. Burn a white candle and draw a circle (chalk is fine) on the cloth that is marked with the directions: North, East,

South, and West. (I use a round mirror with N, E, S, and W written in marker at the four directions and place it on my woven silk cloth.) Surround your altar with art—beautiful paintings, images of faeries, and naturescapes—and play some beautiful music.

Now that you are set up, dedicate your space to the faeries and the highest virtues of the faery kingdom. Recite a poem you like, read from a faery book, or write your own tribute to the faeries. Acknowledge the faeries and their world. You can say or do anything that pleases you and that you think will please them. There are four questions you will want to repeat to yourself, write down, or even speak aloud: What do you seek? What do you offer? Who do you honor? How do we proceed? Make sure you have answers for all of your questions. Spend as much time as you can communing with the faeries. Let them know you are welcoming and friendly to them. Have tea with them (make your own). The rest is up to you. Be creative, get out some paints, make something fun.

Sometimes I like to welcome them in and sit down with my cat, a book, and a cup of pu'erh tea. There is always light, melodic music playing and often a gentle breeze. At times I feel their presence, and I always thank them for joining me.

It's a simple, genuine ritual, one that is usually successful for setting a mood of peace, allowing them to tiptoe in and explore as they choose. In the next chapter, we're going to create a garden for our faery friends; a sanctuary to honor them, nature, and the beauty all around us.

CHAPTER EIGHT

Favorite Faery Flowers, Herbs, and Trees for Gardens

G ardens answer the innate call within us to reach out in celebration of the beauty that surrounds us. We can lose ourselves in the peace and tranquility of a garden space and connect with other realms. When we are enveloped by beautiful things, our souls rejoice in experiencing a haven that restores our very being. By creating a garden sanctuary, we establish a deep connection to nature, the cosmos, and creation itself. It is an outdoor retreat that speaks eloquently to our inner presence. It doesn't matter how big or lavish it is; whether it is a corner, a porch, a windowsill, or an acre of land, it can become magnificent and bloom with beauty. If you have a small space, incorporate crystals and mirrors; if you have a large plot of land, have a ball planting a variety of plants, flowers, trees, and shrubs. You can get lost in this refuge of sweet aromas, bursting color, and stillness. Place a bench in the middle to enjoy the glory. You can add a water feature or natural furniture and enjoy your slice of heaven on earth. When you create a garden, it is a sanctuary and it becomes a beacon for faeries.

Faeries love plants. They are attracted to plants, which they feel sing to them. The songs come in the form of color, shape, size, and accessibility, all of which means that the flowering plants should look joyful, be colorful, smell good, and be close enough to the ground so faeries can dance around them. Flowering plants that attract butterflies, bees, and birds are what faeries love the most. If you would like to find out your special astrological sign flower, see the resource page at the back of the book for a link. Here are some the faery favorites for the garden:

Twelve Flowering Plants Faeries Adore

- Bee Balm (*Monarda didyma*)
- Bluebells (*Hyacinthoides non-scripta*)
- Fuschia (*Fuchsia magellanica*)
- Honeysuckle (*Lonicera*)
- Marigold (*Tagetes*)
- Nasturtium (*Tropaeolum Majus*)
- Pansy (*Viola* × *Wittrockiana*)
- Primrose (*Oenothera*)
- Purple Foxglove (*Digitalis purpurea*)
- Rose (*Rosa*)
- Snapdragon (*Antirrhinum majus*)
- Violets (*Viola*)

Faeries love to frolic in the garden among the herbs and flowers, smelling the fresh fragrance of each bloom. When you enter a garden and you get a feeling of calm and happiness, you can be sure that faeries are present; the sweeter the scents and the bolder the blooms, the more faeries.

Bee Balm (*Monarda didyma*) is one of those plants buzzing with nature. While it was not found in England or Ireland during the 1500 BCE era of the Milesian invasion, it is native to the United States and grows well here. It is faery-approved because it attracts the bees and butterflies they love and it has healing medicinal qualities. You can make a wonderful soothing salve from Bee Balm blossoms and some

Favorite Faery Flowers, Herbs, and Trees for Gardens

beeswax. Bee Balm essential oil and beeswax are available in stores and online.

Bluebells (*Hyacinthoides non-scripta*) are highly popular with the faeries. They have a beautiful, sweet smell and attain thick and luscious growth in wooded areas. Certain areas in the UK have been named "bluebell woods" because the bluebells are so dense that they blanket the forest floor like a carpet. Bluebells flower in early spring and grow exceptionally well in the deep dark woodland where faeries thrive and play. When you plant them in your garden especially for the faeries, they feel very welcomed and "at home." When the faeries party, they can use the flowers as nectar drinking cups by picking them and turning them upside down. The poet Tennyson also attributed them with being a remedy for snake bites.

Fuchsias (*Fuchsia magellanica arsoms*) are colorful, elegant blooming plants that can be hung from pergolas or roofs or strung atop faery gates. They are magnificent in their sweeping majesty and easy for the faeries to dance under and sniff. Although they are not as fragrant as some flowers, there is a color available for everyone's taste and they come in a rainbow of choices except blue. The additional benefit of fuchsias is that their blossoms are edible. Culinary experts say the berries are delicious. The berry fruits of *Fuchsia magellanica* range from maroon to black or blue-black in color and bring a subtle grape flavor with a slight black pepper note. Jams and jellies can be made from fuchsia berries. Can you imagine how excited the faery folk would be if you made them fuchsia berry jelly and spread it on a scone?

Honeysuckle (*Lonicera*) is another beautiful flowering plant that attracts faeries. It can grow as a climbing vine or a bush, and it produces sweet smelling and sweet tasting flowers that will whet faery taste buds. The flowers abound in diverse shades: bright pinks, oranges, yellows, and whites, and some even have a two-colored blossom. Honeysuckle is a romantic flower that has draped many a faery wedding bower. Recipes abound for honeysuckle wine, which is consumed in the summertime at seasonal events. It would be a perfect beverage for a Maypole celebration as well as at the Summer Solstice. Faeries would attend for sure.

HONEYSUCKLE

Marigold (*Tagetes*) is a flower every faery would want in their gardens as a medicinal plant. Marigold has been used in preparations to heal cuts, sores, and anything skin related. Marigold has anti-inflammatory properties and a high concentration of flavonoids like carotene. A salve or a balm made with marigold petals can sooth and heal irritated and traumatized skin. Besides being a vividly bright orange and yellow flower, marigold has ruffled blossoms that dance in the sun. The scented variety of marigold can ward off insects and other predators from the garden. It's a multipurpose plant that brings healing and joy to any garden.

Nasturtium (*Tropaeolum Majus*) is a bonus in any garden and for any gardener regardless of skill level. They come in beautiful bold colors, and, although they are listed as annuals, they do reseed themselves and return year after year. Their leaves and blossoms are edible, and they possess medicinal qualities. They are forgiving plants that make even the first-time gardener look like a pro. They are versatile and do well in regular gardens, rock gardens, pots, hanging arrangements, along sidewalks and, of course, in your faery garden. They are drought tolerant; they can live in poor soil and will even replenish it with plant nutrients. Nasturtiums attract bees and pollinators as well as repel insects. No garden should be without them.

Here's a little recipe for *Nasturtium Tea* (Faeries love it!):

1. Pick one cup of nasturtium flowers, leaves, and buds.

2. Place the flowers in a glass container and gently pour four cups of boiling water over them. Wait eight to ten hours for the brew to steep. Strain and use as you choose over ice or heated as a beverage. Two drops of honey will sweeten the treat.

Pansy (*Viola tricolor var. hortensis*) is the name given to the tricolor wildflower Viola found in Europe, also known as Heartsease. When you look at the beautiful pansy, it does bring ease to your heart. In ancient Greece, if a person was angry, he was given a decoction of pansy. Pansy contains mildly sedative qualities and could ease a headache according to Pliny the Elder. Pansy contains salicylic acid, which is found in aspirin. Pansy also contains small amounts of an anti-inflammatory which can help with respiratory conditions.

Pansy is not just a pretty face. It looks and feels like velvet and brings a certain joy to the heart. In Victorian England, if you received a gift of pansies, it meant someone was interested in you romantically. The faeries love pansies because they grow close to the ground, are colorful, display unlimited variations of hue and pattern, and ease the head and the heart from pain. Your garden should have several pansy plants to spread the joy and ease the pain.

Primrose (*Primula vulgaris*) is a favorite of the faery folk because it comes in four hundred varieties. They grow wildly in the wooded areas and tucked into the forest floor, where they make a delightful surprise for any walker. They prefer afternoon shade, but then, don't we all? Primroses may grow by themselves, in clusters, or in tiers. Some bloom in late winter, others in spring and summer. They cannot survive in a desert, but with proper soil and water, they can be a faithful friend nearly everywhere else. Primrose roots can be harvested after two or three years and made into an infusion as a remedy against headaches. Ointments and balms made from primrose can help skin wounds heal. Line a walkway with primroses, and you will have your own personal primrose path and, very likely, some faery folk.

Purple Foxglove (*Digitalis purpurea*). This plant is tall with little bell-like blossoms hanging off the stem. It is said its name came from the idea that in the forest, foxes can pick and use the blossoms for gloves. Faeries can use the blossoms as drinking horns if they tip them upside down. Foxglove is not a plant you want to ingest. If taken internally, it can cause pain and dizziness. If taken in a large amount, it can result in death. When handling foxglove, wear gloves because the toxins can penetrate your skin. The foxglove plant contains digoxin, a heart medicine which is used to treat heart failure and atrial fibrillation. However, leave the pharmaceuticals to the experts, self-medication could be fatal.

Foxglove should be enjoyed for its elegant three-to-five-foot stems, color, and fairyland appearance. Bees adore the blossoms because they can hide in the blossoms during cold, wind, and rain. Foxglove provides shelter from the storm for many insects. Faeries love to cavort around the foxglove because they have an inherent danger/benefit quality that makes them exciting and dangerous. Do be careful not to allow dogs or cats near these plants as they are poisonous.

Rose (*Rosa*). According to fossil findings, the beautiful and exquisite rose is over thirty-five million years old. It comes in 150 species, and botanical cultivation of roses began five thousand years ago in China. Essential oil was pressed from rose petals in 2000 BCE in the Middle East. Of course faeries love roses because their aroma permeates faery houses and scents their gardens, and faeries can sleep very comfortably on a bed of rose petals. For healing purposes, rose petals have properties that are sedative, anti-inflammatory, antiseptic, and anti-parasitic. Due to roses' antiseptic quality, rose petals crushed into a salve make a wonderful healing balm for bruises, rashes, and some minor wounds. Above all, roses are romantic and elegant and provide exceptional beauty as they expand from buds to open flowers. They are cherished worldwide as one of nature's finest gifts, and faeries find them enchanting and love to be around them.

Snapdragons (*Antirrhinum majus*) are entertaining flowers. Faeries love to play with them because they have little faces like a dragon and when you squeeze them you can make their mouths open and shut. They are a source of great enjoyment and laughter for faeries, who can spend hours playing with snapdragons. Dried snapdragon flowers can be used in poultices to reduce swelling of tumors and hemorrhoids. They can be useful to reduce all kinds of inflammation, including that due to liver disease. Snapdragons grow on walls and in sandy soil and crevices. Planted in a garden, they grow two feet tall and come in colors as deep as crimson and as pale as wheat. Those blossoms feature entertainment value as well as beauty and healing properties, making them necessary for every faery garden.

Violets (*Viola*). Violets are the sacred flower of Faeries. Both wild violets (*Viola odorata*) and violets (*Viola*) can be grown outdoors, whereas African violets are best kept indoors and are not suitable for a faery garden. Wild violets have heart-shaped leaves with purple-blue flowers. Other varieties can have white or yellow blossoms. One of the most delightful gifts wild violets bring is that they often self-seed, returning each year in unexpected locations. It doesn't get more faery perfect than that!

Favorite Faery Flowers, Herbs, and Trees for Gardens

Twelve Herbs That Faeries Treasure

Herbs are used by healers to treat all types of wounds, burns, scrapes, and internal and external complaints and have been effective for centuries before the onset of modern medicine. Plant materials from a myriad of sources have graced the medicine cabinet of many a folk healer and physician since the time of Hippocrates. It's not a surprise then that faeries love herbs for their aroma, healing properties, and food flavorings. If you would like to learn which herbs fit your astrological sign, check out the resource section provided in the back of the book for a link. Here is a list of the herbs faeries love to have growing in their gardens.

- Aloe Vera (*Aloe barbadensis miller*)
- Basil (*Ocimum basilicum*)
- Heather (*Calluna*)
- Lavender (*Lavandula*)
- Mint (*Mentha*)
- Red Valerian (*Centranthus ruber*)
- Rosemary (*Salvia rosmarinus*)
- Saffron (*Crocus sativus*)
- St. John's Wort (*Hypericum perforatum*)
- Thyme (*Thymus vulgaris*)
- Vervain (*Verbena*)
- Yarrow (*Achillea Sibiricaa*)

Plant these herbs for your faery folk in your garden if you can. You'll see why in the descriptions below.

Aloe Vera (*Aloe barbadensis miller*) is called a universal healer because it can help with issues of the skin, burns, wounds, cuts, bruising, and swelling, and, when liquefied, it can assist with digestion, oral health, and acne.

Basil (*Ocimum basilicum*) is a heavenly herb to use in cooking, and it can also help with stomach ailments, intestinal gas, fluid retention and kidney disorders, and head colds. It has also been used to treat warts, insect stings, and snake bites. The leaves are bright green and are soft to the touch.

Heather (*Calluna*) comes from Scotland and grows wild. Purple heather is the most common one, while white is the rarest. Heather is used as a love token from a suitor as well as being harvested for reeds for weaving, making baskets, and thatching. Legend has it that heather will only grow on ground where blood has not been split, and it is also believed that heather grows over the graves of faeries. It is lush, plentiful, and waves romantically in the wind.

Lavender (*Lavandula*) is most certainly at the top of any healer's medicine list. It is antimicrobial, antibacterial, antifungal, anticonvulsant, and a relaxant. It can treat a host of ailments ranging from burns, wounds, cuts, and abrasions to headaches, anxiety, the blues, insomnia, and nausea. It has a beautiful, floral aroma which increases alpha waves in the brain and induces calm. It was used in ancient times in the wash to bring a fresh scent to dirty clothing during the washing process.

Mint (*Mentha*) has been used for centuries to calm an upset stomach, whiten teeth, and freshen a stale mouth. It also has a practical use as an insect repellent and is a prolific plant for any garden. The leaves can be used as a tea, in beverages, and as a flavoring for food. There are hundreds of varieties, but you might be most familiar with spearmint, peppermint, chocolate mint, pineapple mint, apple mint, orange mint, and Swiss mint. Mint is a refreshing stimulant used to counter body fatigue and a tired mind. Mint was named after a Greek nymph who fell in love with Pluto. His wife Persephone discovered the affair and turned the nymph, Mentha, into a plant. Pluto made sure she was sweet smelling and could freshen any air space. (Special note: Persephone herself might have been a faery, since she lived half her year in the underworld.)

MINT

Red Valerian (*Centranthus ruber*) is used to induce sleep and relaxation. The plant can be eaten, stem, blossoms, roots, and all. It is also called Jupiter's beard. It is hardy, grows to three inches in height, and is useful for preventing soil erosion. It is an excellent plant for attracting butterflies.

Rosemary (*Salvia rosmarinus*) is named for the dew *of the sea*. It is astringent, analgesic, diuretic, anti-rheumatic, and can help with congestion. Rosemary has a beautiful aroma and flavors food beautifully. The branches have been used to cook, smoke, and preserve foods. Rosemary has also been worn in weddings and other religious ceremonies as a blessing.

Saffron (*Crocus sativus*) Saffron has been used as a dye, a flavoring, and a medicine. It is cultivated from the dried stigma of the crocus sativus flower. Legend says Cleopatra used it in her bath for the coloring it gave her skin. Saffron threads were woven into ancient carpets and used as a pigment for ancient arts. It is a flavoring often found in Mediterranean dishes. There was a Saffron War in the fourteenth century revolving around the theft of a large shipment of saffron bound for Basel, Switzerland. It is believed to be an antioxidant, aphrodisiac, appetite inhibitor, and is thought to have anti-cancer properties.

St. John's Wort (*Hypericum perforatum*) *was* named for the feast day of St. John on June 24. It has anti-inflammatory, antiviral, and antioxidant healing properties. Paracelsus used it for magic potions and treatments. It was said to protect humans against witches and demons. History notes that the Roman military doctor Proscurides used it in the first century CE. In numerous double-blind clinical trials against a placebo and other antidepressants, the whole extract of St. John's wort, as is found in Jarsin brand coated tablets, has been proven to be just as effective as pharmaceutical antidepressants for mild and moderate depression, but not for severe depression.

Thyme (*Thymus vulgaris*) is a member of the mint family with outstanding healing properties: It is antibacterial, antiviral, antispasmodic, and a stimulant. Ancient Egyptians used thyme for embalming, and the Greeks burned the herb outside temples for purification. Thyme is thought to come from the Greek word *thumos*, meaning "smoke." It is believed to be an antidote to poison. Traditionally, young maidens put it under their pillows to dream of their intended.

Vervain (*Verbena*) is known as *herba sacra* because both the Greeks and Romans used it to purify and sanctify their temples. Though it is a scentless herb, it possesses anti-inflammatory, antibacterial, antispasmodic, and analgesic properties which make it popular for growing, harvesting, and using for healing.

Yarrow (*Achillea Sibiricaa*) has been found in ancient Neanderthal burial sites in Iraq that date back to 60,000 BCE. It has been in use by humans and faeries since then. It has also been used in several wars to stop the bleeding of wounded soldiers, and it has been used to lower blood pressure and regulate blood flow. It was a sacred herb of the Saxons and has also been utilized for flavoring teas and beverages.

Please note that for many of these applications, these herbs should only be used under the supervisions of a naturopath or certified herbal healer.

Twelve Trees That Speak to the Faery Heart

Trees were sacred to the ancient Celts. Trees had medicinal value; they also offered protection against invaders and evil spirits. They were the living abodes for many nature spirits, and the Celts believed they held the power of purification. The tree was the center of many ceremonies and rituals. Most sacred were the ash, hawthorn, and oak. Celtic astrology has a list of twelve trees; you may want to find out which is your tree according to your date of birth. I have provided a resource section in the back of the book with a link for further research.

- Apple (*Malus domestica*)
- Ash (*Fraxinus*)
- Blackthorn (*Prunus spinosa*)
- Cherry Blossom (*Prunus serrulata*)
- Elder (*Sambucus*)
- Elm (*Ulmus*)
- Hawthorn (*Crataegus*)
- Holly (*Ilex*)
- Oak (*Quercus*)
- Rowan (*Sorbus subg. Sorbus*)
- Willow (*Salix*)
- Yew (*Taxus baccata*)

Apple (*Malus domestica*) is a wonderful tree to have in an orchard or backyard. It bears beautiful fruit that can be eaten right off the tree, cooked, or juiced. Apples come in 7,500 varieties and are considered a happy fruit. Some are sweet, some sour, and some are tart, but only some are crabby. Crabapples don't really have a personality but were so named because of their astringent or sour taste from the Swedish word *krabbäple*. Interestingly, apples are related to raspberries, cherries, and strawberries. Apples have excellent health benefits, including heart support, promotion of good gut bacteria, and lowering diabetes risk. They assist with weight loss and may even help prevent some types of cancer. All that in a little round fruit ball! Plus, they are shiny, and faeries love shiny things.

Ash (*Fraxinus*) trees come in colors; you can plant a black, blue, or white ash tree. There are thirteen species of ash, and the ancients used the bark for different color dyes. The blue ash was of course used for blue. The ash tree is related to olive and lilac trees. Ash is a faery favorite because the branches grow opposite each other, creating a nice balance on the trunk. The young supple branches can be used for weaving baskets. Ash trees produce winged seeds that delight the faeries because they look like little angels hanging upside down on the branches. The ash tree provides lovely shade from the sun without blocking out all of the rays. It is the tree called *Yggdrasil* in Norse lore.

Blackthorn (*Prunus spinosa*), also known as sloe, is so many things to so many! First of all, it is in the rose family. It bears thorns and fruit; the fruit has been used to flavor sloe gin or flavored wines for centuries, and the Irish use the wood to make their *shillelaghs*, traditionally employed as cudgels as well as walking sticks. The blackthorn makes spiky thorns that can be pulled off the branch and used as little swords for play or defense if needed. The bush grows into excellent hedges and makes beautiful corrals for livestock. The wood burns warm and smokeless, so it is a favorite for the underground living faerie folk.

Cherry Blossom (*Prunus serrulata*) is a very special tree to the faeries because when the pink blossoms fall, the faeries dance enthusiastically around in the pink "snow." The cherry blossoms pop out in the spring, symbolizing renewal and the ephemeral joy of new life. The blossoms are edible and frequently pickled with leaves in a mixture of salt and vinegar and used with certain foods to bring out the flavor. The fragrance comes from the substance coumarin, which is found in the leaves. Coumarin is used as a blood thinner for heart patients, so beware; it is highly advisable to stay on the conservative side of eating cherry blossoms. It's best to be faery-like and enjoy the beauty and the delicacy of the blossoms by dancing around on them as they form a carpet of pink under the tree.

CHERRY BLOSSOM

Elder (*Sambucus*). Oh, the exquisite elderberry, the provider of natural dyes in vibrant colors and delicious drinks and jams. To ward off an enemy, a faery might pick some elder berries, press them into fresh juice, and serve it to the foe. The guest may double over in agony, retching and crying out in pain, thereby losing the battle before it even began. Elderberries are toxic when eaten raw or uncooked. But cooked and steeped, they make beautiful teas, wines, drinks, and desserts. Elderberries are rich in anthocyanins, giving them their beautiful red, black, and purple color. Elderberry contains antioxidants and anti-inflammatory agents and could be an important part of the faeries' medicinal garden.

Elm (*Ulmus*). The elm tree is associated with death and the Underworld. Elm wood has long been considered useful for building boats because it withstands water very well. Archers have made sturdy longbows from the supple wood. Elm branches have been known to fall onto the head of an unsuspecting passerby, thereby clinching the tree's connection to death. Due to its association with the Underworld and the afterlife, coffins were frequently made from elm. Oddly enough, it was a favorite tree of the early Celts, as they performed their May Day celebrations around the village elm. It is the tree that brings hope: hope to sail to a new land, and hope for a resurrection, since the elm has been plagued with Dutch elm disease almost to the point of extinction. Today, however, new techniques for tree cloning foster the possibility of bringing back the sweeping elegance of the elm tree to once again grace our gardens and delight the faeries.

Hawthorn (*Crataegus*). Here is a lovely tree with red berries to delight the birds and insects of the forest. Hawthorns are hardy trees; they are not much of a problem to cultivate and can grow anywhere there is a rock or crevice. Over two hundred species of insect and bird life depend on this tree for nourishment and shelter. It is also used for hedges and can be trimmed to hold a shape. If you find a lone hawthorn tree in the middle of a field, you have come across a faery tree. It is bad luck to cut it down, and, in Ireland, engineers will create a path around the tree to avoid damaging it for fear of bad luck and upsetting the faery folk. A faery tree is a gateway and a portal between the worlds of mortals and the immortals.

Some healers have attributed anti-inflammatory qualities to hawthorn, as well as properties that help with controlling blood pressure, atherosclerosis, and heart disease. In Chinese medicine, it is a key remedy for digestion and cholesterol reduction. You may have noticed that many of the plants faeries love have benefits for the heart. Since it is the main organ for keeping humans alive, perhaps it is a message from the faery world to keep our hearts healthy and in good working order.

Holly (*Ilex*). Just like the hawthorn, holly produces red berries. In fact, holly is used in annual celebrations worldwide and has been a sacred offering for centuries. Holly was the official headdress of the Druid priests when they went into the woods for prayer and ceremony. The ancient Romans offered holly branches to the god Saturn during his feast days at the Winter Solstice. The holly tree was used to mark the coming of winter and was the precursor of the common Christmas tree we see today. The wood of the holly tree is very hard, making it suitable for durable goods like furniture. The waxy, shiny, bright green leaves attract the artist's eye. Holly berries are fine for birds and animals, but toxic to humans. It has been used as a symbol of good luck and prosperity for ages. I would think the faeries pick the holly leaves and place them as a bower over their gold as a way to increase and protect it.

Oak (*Quercus*). The faeries probably had a hand in writing the song "Tie a Yellow Ribbon Round the Old Oak Tree," because that is exactly what they would have done. The oak tree is one of the most treasured and beloved trees in the world. It represents strength, wisdom, morality, and resistance. The mighty oak has been a source of life for humankind since the beginning of time. Oak trees predate humans and faeries in this world as they have been around for sixty-five million years; some have lived for one thousand years. Humans have built ships, homes, meetinghouses, and carriages from oak for as long as anyone can remember. One of the reasons the oak has endured is due to the acorn. Its seed is covered in a hard-to-damage shell, and each large tree can produce 20,000 acorns of which 10,000 will go to seed and perhaps create a new tree. And you guessed it! Faeries love acorns. They can roll them around, sit on them, pile them up, make shelters with them, and turn them into musical instruments. Have you ever heard a band of acorn drummers marching through the underbrush?

Rowan (*Sorbus subg. Sorbus*). The rowan tree is legendary for being the tree on which the first runes were carved. Ancient northern people carried small bits of rowan branches with them as protection and tied them to their livestock to safeguard the beasts. Rowan twigs were used for divining, and the berries were used to dye sacred garments worn in ceremony. Rowan was the wood of choice for tools of the land and implements of battle. Rowan berries were also used for brewing ale, wine and spirits. Burning the wood of the rowan tree was not allowed except for in sacred ceremonies because it was revered and considered to have magical qualities. The faeries treasure rowan trees. They gather around them at special times of the year: the Winter and Summer Solstices, the Spring and Autumnal Equinoxes, Beltane (May Day), Samhain (Halloween), Lughnasa (feast of the first fruits of harvest), and Imbolc (Candlemas), the traditional Celtic celebrations tied to the seasons and the movements of the sun and moon.

Willow (*Salix*). There may not be a more gracious and elegant tree than the willow. The wood of the willow is used in making musical instruments, baskets, and furniture. Willow bark contains salicylic acid, which healers use for headaches, toothaches, and fever. Willow is associated with regeneration and fertility. The trees are also a symbol of survival, resilience, and reemergence because of the way the willow branches bend in the winds. Willows are strong trees and root easily. They are sturdy yet flexible, with their ability to bend without breaking. They grow eight feet of height per year and will form a strong presence in relation to the land where they are planted. Faeries love willow trees because it is fun to swing and play on the branches and they can use the supple limbs to make many a wondrous arch, swing, or roof covering. Many a faery wedding has taken place under the wispy boughs of the weeping willow tree.

Yew (*Taxus baccata*). This legendary tree has been known to live for three thousand years. It is used to shield the living against spells and as a protector of the dead. Taxol is a medicinal substance found in the yew tree that is now being used to treat several types of cancer. Yew trees have very hard-coated seeds and so are dependent on birds to release their seeds from their husks so they can sprout. The yew tree has been overharvested and is now a protected species so it can proliferate in a sustainable way. The leaves and other parts of the tree are highly poisonous to humans and animals, so farmers need to take care where they allow their animals to graze and make sure it is not too close to the yews. The wood is hard and used for bow making. An arrowhead made from yew has been found to date back 450,000 years. Yew may be the oldest living tree on the earth. The faeries are honored to preserve it for future generations to enjoy, but not deplete.

Your Faery Garden

Setting up a faery garden is a sacred appointment. Never begin setting up a garden for faeries if you are angry or upset. Put yourself in the right frame of mind first. Meditate, listen to uplifting music, find peace within, and then begin to create a garden suitable for a faery. Make sure that your gardening tools are clean and your soil is fresh and supplemented with rich loam or compost. Consider this task to be a function of the three worlds coming together to honor the faery kingdom: the Air and Sky of the Upperworld, the earth, soil, and plants of the Middleworld, and the water, roots, and minerals of the Lowerworld.

Select your plants, prepare your soil, and draw a schematic of your garden. It's not important if you have a large or small space. What matters most is that you have room for a stone circle for faery dancing, a faery door or gate, colorful plants that bloom, items that sparkle, and herbs that please the faery heart. Count out your plants, work in threes, and arrange them as you would like to see the color palette in bloom. Section out space for a faery circle, a faery gate or door, and whatever ornaments you want to have for them. The addition of a little table and chairs is a nice touch, and some faery garden designers also enjoy placing ceramic toadstools or small bowls they can fill with water. I've even seen some elaborate faery gardens with tiny stones, bridges, pathways, and miniature circulating fountains. You don't have to go all out, but at minimum, a faery gate and a stone circle are important.

Faery gates are things you can buy online or make yourself; I have several. One is a gate I purchased and painted. The door came in brown and I painted it a metallic purple. I also painted the wings on the faerie icon that came molded to the door gold, and I gave her bright green grass to walk on. The other is more like a wrought iron gate with an over-piece. It was a part of some leftover garden fencing that I sprayed purple, and then hung crystal ornaments on the sides.

In front of the gates, I set up a faery circle of stones. I choose twelve roundish stones and one special agate for the center. When the stones get wet, their colors come out, so I made sure they are near a sprinkler head where they can shine brightly with all their visual qualities a few times a week. I even made a little table for them of Popsicle sticks and propped it up on a flat rock. I gathered a few more rocks and placed them around the table as seats for faery visitors. I leave a little bit of honey in a small bowl (a sake cup) as an offering to them. I bought them a stone wishing well, and I do my best to keep it filled with fresh water. Sometimes thirsty birds give me a challenge. My faery area is located amongst roses, thyme, marigolds, pansies, violets, and assorted purple flowers. The area is shaded by a Ficus tree and a staghorn fern, so, even in Southern California, they can feel like they are in the woods.

My Faery Gate.

My Faery Stone Circle.

Favorite Faery Flowers, Herbs, and Trees for Gardens

You don't need to have an elaborate gate, but you'll want to create some type of designated area that welcomes them into your physical space. Faeries are known for making grand entrances.

Once you have sketched out your garden space, leaving ample room for faery areas, you can begin to plant. Check the amount of space each plant will need when it is full grown (you can find botanical information online) and plant your plants accordingly. Make sure you have a water source for your plants; either acquire an automated sprinkler system or mark your calendar for hand-watering days.

When you are planting your faery garden, give consideration to how it will look in the moonlight. Faeries will be out to play, and you want them to be able to enjoy the moonlight as well as the daylight. I have some small solar lights that are round and look like the moon. They seem to really enjoy playing around and sitting on those globe fixtures.

One of the sweetest lessons I learned about planting flowers and gardens was from the first gardener I ever hired. I couldn't afford him every week, so he agreed to come help me with my property every other week. When I could, I spent time with him, working side by side. His name was Mr. Ramos, and he was the kind of person who absolutely loved what he did. His hands were soft, and his fingers were long and slim. He looked like he played piano for a living rather than working the earth.

When I bought my first house, it was a bank-owned foreclosure and had not been looked after for six or seven months. The grass had turned brown, the weeds were five feet high, and what plants remained were sunburned and crisp. There were twenty-two trees on the land, but they were in various stages of death and dying. Mr. Ramos saw me standing in the yard with my gardening gloves on from across the street. He literally came out of nowhere, walked over casually, smiling, and asked me, "Do you need a gardener?" I told him I needed a miracle. He laughed and told me he could come every week and help me get control of the wild landscape outside my front door. We settled on every other week, and, little by little, Mr. Ramos and I got it all under control with the help of hoses, weed whackers, shovels, and a lot of topsoil.

I couldn't believe it when Mr. Ramos said he could "bring back" a lot of the plants and trees. He pruned back some crispy branches and told me they would flower in the spring. He pruned the trees almost down to the bone, affirming that they would fruit again. In the flower beds next to the house, we planted new gardenias, birds of paradise, and impatiens in bright colors. It seemed that every time he touched something, it sprang back to life. I loved to watch him in the garden. He sat back on his heels like an elf on the grass or soil beds, smiling and humming a quiet tune to himself.

Each time we put a new plant in the earth, Mr. Ramos created a circle of raised dirt around the plant. I asked him why he did that, and he said, "It keeps the water around the plant roots and it keeps them safe." Years later, I learned that he was creating circles of protection, faery circles, around each one so they would stay healthy and safe. He was right. All of the fruit trees bore fruit, and the brown crispy stems in the garden turned out to be gorgeous purple and red fuchsias; they created wispy limbs of abundant blossoms bursting with color that made the house look like a palace.

Favorite Faery Flowers, Herbs, and Trees for Gardens

Mr. Ramos was a blessing to the land, and I cried the day he told me he was going to retire. He couldn't bend easily anymore, and his hands were getting stiff. What had been a joy to him had become difficult and painful, so he had to stop. Mr. Ramos helped me with my gardens for twenty years, and those were the nicest years my gardens and I could have ever asked for. Every time I plant a new flower, I think of Mr. Ramos. When I create a faery ring around each one, I send him a little blessing and ask the faeries to watch out for him, wherever he is. He may actually have been a faery come to help me. It's a pleasant thought.

When you plant your plants, surround them with a small circle of dirt. The circle should be about six to eight inches away from the trunk, and it only needs to be two inches high, just enough to keep the water in and allow it to soak into the roots.

If some of your plants are annuals, you will need to take out the dead remains and replant them next season. Try to keep your garden current and free of weeds and dead plants. Clip out dead branches to make way for new growth. Pinch off dead blossoms to make way for new flowers. Read up on how to grow and care for the plants you choose to have in your faery garden. The time you spend caring for your garden will be appreciated. Faeries like gardens to be tidy and clean. If your garden becomes overgrown and unkempt, you may be in for some mischief. We certainly wouldn't want that!

Have you ever walked in a botanical garden? How did you feel? Have you seen or experienced the beauty of true English style gardens? They are designed to present an idyllic snapshot of nature, one created with structure and symmetry without being too rigid. Gardens are magical places or can be. They are full of variety, interest, and beauty. Before you begin your faery garden, have a look around the web for different design ideas, and pattern yours after the ones that resonate with you. That will become your ideal and perfect faery garden.

Which flowers, plants, trees, and herbs will you use for your faery garden? In the next chapters, we'll learn about the crystals and essential oils that faeries love and find attractive.

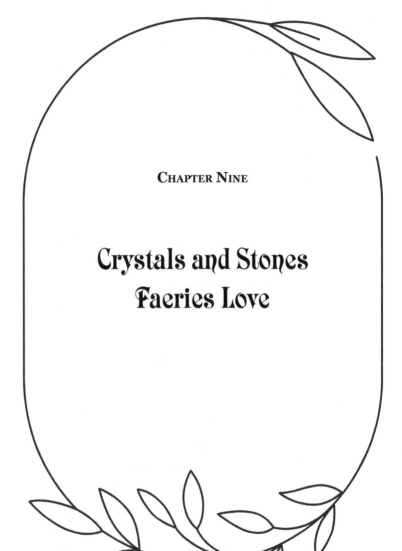

CHAPTER NINE

Crystals and Stones Faeries Love

Well, of course, faeries love crystals. They are beautiful, they sparkle, they hold secrets, and they contain magic. Remember when we talked about faeries loving order? Well, that's one of the other reasons they love crystals. Crystals are extremely organized groupings of atoms arranged in a highly ordered microscopic configuration. This organization follows a repeating lattice pattern, and that's why crystals are an efficient substance for transmitting energy, heat, and light from one place to another. Quartz crystal is used often by modern industry because of its stability and reliability in conducting and transmitting electromagnetic energy. It's the perfect substance, and that is why quartz crystals are used in electronics, computers, cell phones, and laser surgery. Quartz crystal contains 46 percent silicon and 53 percent oxygen, and it is the second most abundant mineral on earth next to feldspar. Abundant, sparkly, and beautiful—the perfect adornment for a faery.

Every civilization has utilized quartz crystal in some manner. In ancient China circa 5000 BCE, crystals and gemstones were used in classic Chinese medicine for healing the ailing meridians of the body. The Sumerians used them in their magic formulas in the fourth millennium BCE. In India, according to the Ayurvedic tradition, crystals were used for healing as early as 1000 BCE. In South America, hand-carved crystal talismans were used in ancient religious ceremonies and worship. King Tutankhamen (1324 BCE) was buried with a death mask containing quartz, turquoise, lapis lazuli, obsidian, feldspar, amazonite, and other gemstones for power and protection on his journey in the afterlife. The ancient Egyptians prized crystal jewelry as much for its healing power as for its decorative beauty.

Crystals contain minerals that can help heal faeries and humans when used correctly and with directed intention. Crystals are alive and contain vibrational patterns of energy that oscillate within and project outwards. Faeries can sit beside them and feel the hum of their power. They have a perfect understanding of what each stone can do and why.

I believe faeries relate best to stones that are associated with the three realms, the Upper, Middle, and Lower worlds. Below is a chart you can refer to in order to identify what stones represent which world and how they relate to the characteristics of the faeries who dwell within them. Faeries will resonate to the stones which correspond to their world. The Upperworld is represented by the element Air; the Middleworld is represent by Earth and Fire; and the Lowerworld is represented by Water. If you want to work with the faeries, here is a suggested list of the crystals that they relate to.

QUARTZ, UPPERWORLD

World	Element	Crystals/Stones
Upperworld	Air	Apophyllite, Prenhite, Clear Quartz, Herkimer Diamond, Amethyst, Celestite, Peridot, Pink Calcite Citrine (associated with the sun) Selenite (associated with the moon)
Middleworld	Earth Fire	Jasper, Carnelian, Shungite, Black Tourmaline, Agate, Green Jade, Preseli Bluestone, Petrified wood Ruby, Garnet, Sardonyx, Sunstone, Amber, Fire Agate, Red Tourmaline
Lowerworld	Water	Fluorite, Lapis Lazuli, Chrysocolla, Aquamarine, Apatite, Turquoise, Labradorite

The Upperworld—Air

The first type of crystal you can use to connect with faeries in the Upperworld is **Apophyllite**. It is a stone of resonating attraction that enhances one's personal magnetism and brings others to you. You become irresistible to others when you use this stone's vibration. It assists in cementing relationships, and it is perfect for starting faery friendships! Apophyllite, with its hint of green, reminds us of our connection to nature, which helps to ground the human spirit and guide the soul into a space of calmness and serenity. It is also called the stone of the angels.

Another lovely stone of the Upperworld is **Prenhite**. Prenhite is a stone of unconditional love, healing, and connection. It is usually light green, the color of the heart chakra, and has the qualities of a healer. It calms environments, encourages peace, and elicits protection. Prenhite establishes harmony and heightens inner knowing. It dissolves fears and barriers and sets a welcoming and accepting atmosphere for all natural elements. It also works well for dream cycles and remembering dreams. Prenhite establishes an effective path for contacting faeries through your dreams so they can manifest in the ordinary world.

Faeries relate to **Clear Quartz** crystal, which is also known as the universal healer stone. It is imbued with the qualities of a master healer and is considered by many to be the incarnation of divine cosmic energy. Faeries love the purity of the stone, its clarity, and the fact that it is full of energy and light. Some stones are clear while others have occlusions and crackles inside that catch the light and make rainbows. In the faery world, the rainbow is a blessing.

Another stone faeries love is the **Herkimer Diamond**. It has been termed the most powerful of all the quartz crystals, because each is double terminated with points on either side; Herkimer diamonds are short and stubby and much harder than regular quartz. They sparkle like diamonds and are nearly as strong. These stones are excellent for the attunement of one being to another—and therefore perfect for faery work. They also clear environments of negative energy, pollution, and stuck or stagnant energy patterns. Herkimer diamonds can easily be programmed to hold and retain positive emotions, affirmations, and the vibration of love, and such an imprint can be stored for long periods of time. It may be small in size, but it packs a mighty power. Be sure to get two, one for you and one for your faery friend. That way you can connect through the vibrations of the Upperworld and the Middleworld with ease.

Amethyst comes in shades ranging from deep purple to pale lavender and is a high vibration stone. It's been called "Nature's tranquilizer" and is a master stone for healers. Amethyst connects the vibrations of heaven and earth, the realms of the seen and the unseen. It builds strengths, enhances purpose, increases intellectual ability, and enhances serenity and composure. It's probably best known for its ability to open the channels of psychic connection and clairvoyance. It is a wonderful stone for opening the faery worlds and connecting to them in the right frame of mind and spirit of exchange.

Celestite is another heavenly stone. It is a perfect stone for meditation and inducing dreams that solve problems and answer questions. Like amethyst, celestite helps you tap into your psychic abilities and sharpen your intuition. If you receive information from the spiritual world it helps those messages gain expression and clarity in your mind. Celestite is a beautiful stone with a vibration that enhances our awareness of the divine light that exists within all of us, including, and especially, faeries.

Peridot is in the list of Upperworld stones because it is sent from the cosmos to us. The Gem Society of America calls it an "extreme gem" because it is formed in molten rock and brought to the surface through the force of a volcano. Peridot has an extraterrestrial footprint and has even been found on the moon. Thought to have been brought to earth by a solar explosion, peridot embodies incredible healing properties. Since it is green, faeries love it. And since it has cosmic power, we all love it.

Pink Calcite: similar to rose quartz, this is the stone of heart healing, heart connection, love, and healing from emotional traumas and hurts. It's a beautiful stone because it mends heartbreaks and opens the heart for more love by connecting to the highest realms of love and cosmic vibrations of divine love. This stone cleanses, makes room for true love and erases past memories of painful connections. Using pink calcite, you can cleanse your heart and clear the path for a clear and clean relationship with a faery friend.

The sun is represented by **Citrine**, which has been a wildly popular stone for tools, swords, and jewelry and has even been used to decorate palaces. Its name comes from "citron," the French word for a lemon or the color lemon yellow. It has been called the stone of the mind because it is able to transmute negative thinking into positive thinking and increase mental clarity. Citrine is the stone of leadership, and it is one of the very few stones that never needs cleansing; it cleanses itself automatically.

The moon is represented by **Selenite**, the stone of mental clarity, psychic connections, and angels. This stone expands awareness, opens the unconscious, and sheds light on dark secrets. No wonder it represents the moon! It brings meaning to the mysterious and finds the positive in the shadows. It insists on truth, honesty, and clarity and brings peace and harmony to every situation it encounters. It reduces fear and anxiety by attuning to the higher self.

The Middleworld—Earth

Jasper is a stone of vigor, courage, and physical healing. Its nickname is "the supreme nurturer" because it possesses grounding properties like stability and strength. It is also imbued with shamanic wisdom and was carved into amulets of protection by the ancients. Kings, emperors, and pharaohs considered it the ultimate stone of protection in battle and even placed jasper on their horse bridles for additional power. There are many varieties of jasper, and all are related to the energy of the earthly plane.

Carnelian is a stone of creativity and assistance. It's one of the oldest on earth and dates back to at least 4000 BCE. It increases passion and courage and was worn by warriors for motivation in battle. It has been known to protect one's home from fire, theft, and psychic invasion, and it stabilizes the emotions of anger and rage. In ancient Egypt, it signified position and rank in society. Many Egyptians thought that wearing carnelian would protect them from the plague and death in general. Faeries love it for the protection and courage it provides them.

Shungite is a stone found in Russia that has a distinct carbon makeup. (It has abilities to oxidize water and air and rid water of free radicals thirty times greater than carbon due to fullerenes.) The bactericide in the mineral provides anti-pathogen protection, which is why it is used for water purification treatments. Anytime you want to purify something like water, use Elite Noble Shungite, but don't drink the water if you soak any other types of Shungite in it. It could contain other minerals that are not potable. Faeries love Shungite because it comes from a singular place under the earth's crust, and they love that.

Black Tourmaline, also known as *Schorl*, is a grounding stone that absorbs negativity and retains an electrical charge when heated. It is called the great balancer because it is believed that the ridges on its sides connect heaven to earth. It has the ability to dispel doom and gloom by absorbing negative energy, and it can send evil spells right back to the sender, like a boomerang. Faeries like its magical rebounding qualities.

Agate comes in all the colors of the earth. Agate comes from the volcanic center of the earth and is usually banded, striated, or layered. It is rich in earth energy and grounding properties. Agate is the every-person stone. It has a lower vibration, is connected to inner earth, and brings calm and stability to the person who holds it. It is not expensive and is easily found in streams, on beaches, and in places where there are natural rocks and minerals. An agate is frequently the first rock a young person owns. Faeries adore how available it is and use it for building homes and gardens.

Green jade is a very old stone and has been used for healing and décor for millennia. It is associated with abundance, heart love, and balance. There are seven or eight colors of jade, but we've chosen green jade to represent earth and the vibrations we want to reach the Middleworld faeries. Jade is a huge healer and has been used for that purpose all over the world, from ancient civilizations in China, to the Mayans in South America and the Maoris in New Zealand. It is a stone of dreamers and dreaming and aids all healers in their work. It calms, grounds, inspires, and stabilizes emotions. While doing all of that, it is also the stone of good fortune and romance. Faeries love this stone, which is like the earth-muse for them.

Preseli bluestone comes from the Preseli Hills in southwest Wales. The stone is imbued with magical, earthly, and faery vibrations. The ancient Celts liked the vibrations from this stone so much that in 2,500 BCE, they lugged it 150 miles from Wales to build Stonehenge in Somerset, England. The inner circle at Stonehenge was made from eighty single-quarried Preseli bluestones weighing in at two to four tons each. The Celts knew that these stones carried a special heart-centered earth energy that connected them to the cosmos, along with acoustic energy for enhancing sound and music. The Chinese call this *dragon energy*. I have stood in the center of Stonehenge and watched my pendulum leap around like a jumping bean on steroids. I can attest to the power in these stones. Having experienced its energy firsthand, I use Preseli bluestone all the time to ramp up my communication with faeries.

Petrified wood is another great stone that faeries love. It is a stone of transformation that helps you reach your intended and higher level. It helps keep you feeling safe and calm as you make the transition between levels. It is a survival-based stone and can bring serenity and grounding to an anxious moment or one filled with doubt or distrust. It helps you set an even pace without strain or overexertion.

The Middleworld—Fire

Ruby says "fire," as do many of the stones connected to the Middleworld. Ruby represents blood, passion, and life-force energy. In biblical times, when a ruby was pressed into the flesh and worn, it rendered the wearer completely invulnerable. Ruby represents love and restrained lust. It signifies royalty, leadership, and privilege. It is a rare stone, and faeries prize it for its beauty and luster. It is the color of the physical heart and stirs the very core of life's essence.

Garnet is another deep red stone with the qualities of strength, safety, and higher consciousness; for this reason, you'd think it would be in the Upperworld, but it is associated with gratitude and service to others since it is also the color of the heart organ. It has been called the stone of *living fire* because it inspires one to help others. This is a perfect stone and one ideal for the Middleworld because it is here that we are in service to our fellow humans. Faeries are particularly fond of kindness and assistance to others, so they resonate beautifully to this stone and its aura and vibration of compassionate care.

Sardonyx is our next Middleworld gemstone connected to the element of Fire. Sardonyx is another banded stone that brings courage, clear communication, and strength. It dates back to ancient Egypt, where soldiers wore sardonyx rings into battle. In Rome, cameo carvings were created to see the image in white on a warm reddish-brown background. Sardonyx contains truth and hidden courage within the stone. The stone itself is composed of alternating layers of *sard* and *onyx*, hence its name derives from the combination. You can use these stones for bonding with the earth and playing in the other worlds since you have white, black and brown to work with.

Sunstone is another brilliant gem with the vibrant colors of fire and earth. This is a beautiful and happy stone which clears and cleanses all negative energies and restores joy and exuberance. Sunstone is restorative, especially in the case of a major loss, and helps pry away the claws of codependency. It's a freeing stone of liberation and individuality. Like the sun, the wearer can stand alone with shining strength and warmth for all around them. Faeries love sunstone because it warms their souls and brightens their days.

Amber is formed through the fossilization process of tree resin. Since it contains ancient vibrations and perspectives, it is a purifier of mind, body, and spirit, representative of our three worlds. Amber heightens self-confidence and thereby enhances self-expression. Amber wants you to be all you can be and removes emotional blocks so you can succeed. It has the glorious, deep, rich color of the sun and is a manifestation stone for your talents. Call on amber to help you break through the forest into the sunlight, or through an artist's block. Faeries find this stone sacred because it has survived through the ages. They seek its wisdom and knowledge.

Fire agate is the stone of the Hero's Journey, so it promotes courage, strength, and endurance and moves us bravely onto our ultimate spiritual path. If you are contemplating a big change in your life, fire agate is your stone. It encourages vitality while helping to provide stability and grounding. Faeries recognize it as a stone of fire, passion, and fervor. It's a powerful assistant for moving forward with strong mental conviction.

Red Tourmaline is also known as Rubellite. It helps us surrender to divine energies and to follow our call with passion. Other stones pale by comparison to its fierce connection to the heart. Some stones have different hues under different lighting conditions, but not red tourmaline. It shines as brightly and vibrantly in daylight as it does under artificial light. Its radiance shines through no matter what. Needless to say, this is a passionate favorite of the faeries.

The Lowerworld—Water

Fluorite brings clarity, purpose, and order to the Lowerworld. Water needs something to hold it, otherwise it runs all over the place. Fluorite is the vessel to contain water and all of its wonderful qualities of the lower regions. Faeries love fluorite because it has translucent layers of a pastel rainbow and all rainbows bring them blessings.

Lapis Lazuli is a stone of truth, inner power, and organization. Just like Fluorite, Lapis Lazuli provides structure for the amorphous element of water. This stone is reputed to have existed before time began, which makes it as old as water. It guides the mind through altered states and safely back to reality again. It represents both male and female energies, so it is a stone of balance in the watery Underworld of our deepest thoughts, feelings, and beliefs. Faeries respond to this stone because it holds all of the secrets of their lives underground.

Chrysocolla brings tranquility to the watery realm. It balances, calms, cools, and adjusts. It ignites creativity, especially through the heart, and aids the ability to speak the truth in an even and stable manner. This stone balances a physical area as well as the people in it. Chrysocolla washes away fear and replaces those feelings with a sense of well-being and safety. Faeries like feeling safe!

Aquamarine means *water of the sea* and refers to the sparkling color, clarity, and welcoming nature of water. It is wonderful for studying anything new. It increases focus, clarity, intellectual ability, brings intuitive gifts, and even encourages the tolerance and patience one needs when studying a new subject. Aquamarine supports learning abilities and the taking in and assimilation of new information. Aquamarine connects us to mass consciousness, brotherhood, and oneness with all of humanity and of course with the faery realm.

Apatite is the stone you want when you are feeling irritated, unsettled, and out of whack, because it brings calm and eases sorrow. It helps sort through confusion and clears the path for direct movement forward. It encourages the holder to expand their knowledge, concentrate on the greater good, and focus on selfless acts and beliefs. It is a deeply spiritual stone focusing on psychic abilities and intuitive knowledge. Be sure you know what you are buying because other stones pose as apatite and are not. Faeries will help you find the correct stone.

Turquoise brings protection, energy, and serenity all in one lovely stone. Turquoise dates back to pre-Egyptian times and was one of the first stones to be used in making jewelry. It is a stone of friendship that brings people together. It fosters honest communication between two people and is a master stone of unification. Faeries like the feeling of camaraderie it fosters.

Labradorite is a wonderful stone of transformation that assists with the process of change. Change can be a rocky trip, so labradorite stabilizes and grounds all spiritual energies and focuses on the purpose and intention toward shift and upward movement on a spiritual path. Labradorite sees through illusions and forms a clear picture while at the same time strengthening self-love. This stone quells the overactive mind and encourages the gut and the heart to lead the way. Transformation can be lonely but labradorite will see you through and walk by your side. Faeries feel brave when they are around this stone.

Further Notes on Other Stones and Crystals

Certain metaphysical stores carry *faery stones*. These are made of calcium carbonate and are concretions formed at the bottom of lakes, left there by ancient glaciers. They have glob-like shapes, and each one is different. Yes, this is the same chemical calcium carbonate that is used for digestion problems and to remedy calcium deficiency in bones, tissue, and the heart.

$CaCO_3$ is commonly found in pearls, marine organisms, and in snail and eggshells. I suppose these discoveries were dubbed *faery stones* because they have been buried underground or under glaciers for eons. I have not found them to be particularly effective with the faeries I know, but you could always see what they might do for you. I think they are more the object of a marketing ploy than a healing stone.

Another stone that is commonly attributed to faeries is Staurolite, which features a twin stone formation pattern that resembles a cross. This is a fabricated hypothesis which falls apart when you look at faeries historically. They were around long before Christianity and would not have even seen a cross. Therefore, this stone is not related to faeries, it is simply another fantasy of marketing and sales.

What you want to keep in mind when dealing with crystals is connecting to the faery empire using the mineral kingdom as a bridge. Faeries are comfortable with natural elements and these stones are a happy connection for them. The more you know about the essentials of nature, the easier it will be for you to make friends with faeries. They adore plants, they resonate with crystals and gemstones, and they are absolutely head over heels for essential oils. Next, we'll see what they are excited about in that world. Faery essentials!

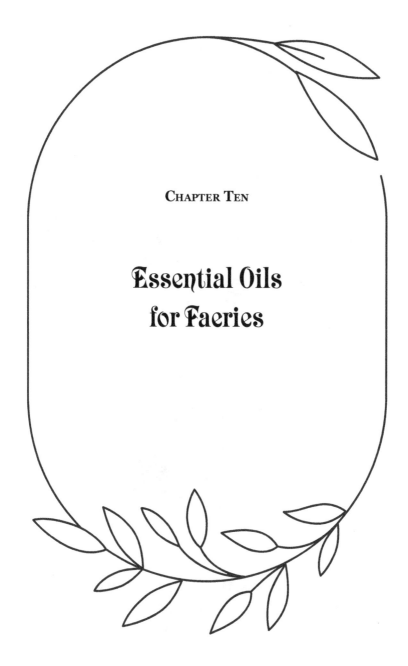

CHAPTER TEN

Essential Oils
for Faeries

aeries are spirits of nature, and because of that, they love plants, flowers, aromas, and a chance to be one with nature as often and as closely as possible. They especially love essential oils, which are the natural products plants themselves create to protect and heal. When their essence is extracted from the plant, humans and faeries can use these natural remedies to heal on the physical, mental, and spiritual planes. "Essential oils are natural because they originate from the global ecosystem; they are valuable because they are noninvasive and do not bombard the body with anything artificial or contain human-made chemical properties; they are complementary to human life because they elevate the whole person while they help to heal; they are considered divine and miraculous by many because they are simple, potent—and some would say even magical—in their uses and effects."

ESSENTIAL OILS

Essential oils can be inhaled by using a diffuser, they can be diluted in a carrier oil and applied to the body, or they can be made into an inhaler or compress, used in the bath, employed on diffuser reeds, or added to existing products to benefit the user. Below is a chart of essential oils that coincide with the three worlds of the faeries. I use them based on their vibration, the effect they have on people and the environment, and the mood they set when exposed to air.

World	Essential Oils
Upper (Air)	Lavender, Lemongrass, Melissa, Peppermint
Middle (Earth) (Fire)	Cypress, Vetiver, Patchouli Basil, Clove, Cedarwood, Frankincense, Nutmeg, Orange
Lower (Water)	Blue Chamomile, Eucalyptus, Jasmine, Myrrh, Sandalwood, Bergamot

The Upperworld—Air

Lavender (*Lavandula*)

If I could select just one essential oil out of all there are in the world, I would have to choose lavender. It has antibacterial and antiviral qualities as well as being sedative and anti-inflammatory. The floral aroma is relaxing and soothing. Faeries love it because it attracts love, and it is said to promote long life with regular use. Its healing properties are legendary.

Lemongrass (*Cymbopogon*)

This essential oil has antidepressant, antiseptic, nervine, and sedative qualities. It can help reduce body pain from strenuous activities, and it can help with viral based infections, coughs, colds, and fever. It is an effective muscle relaxer and oddly enough a pesticide. (It is similar to citronella.) Faeries love it because it is aromatic and fresh and seems to make things happen.

Melissa (*Melissa officinalis*)

Also known as lemon balm, the Greeks named this essential oil for the honeybees. It has a pleasing and sweet scent and is antiviral, antibacterial. and antidepressive. It has an aura of gentleness which appeals to the faeries. It is uplifting and restful and can lighten a sad mood in minutes. It helps with sleep, reduces fatigue, and is an all-around blessing in a bottle. The faeries adore it because it is associated with their friends the bees.

Peppermint (*Mentha × piperita*)

This is a favorite essential oil the world over. It is fresh, clean, and energetic and has stimulant, analgesic, and antispasmodic effects, as well as one of the most cheerful essential oils around. Peppermint can be relied on to boost energy, freshen breath, release tight muscles, reduce fever, and quell an upset stomach. Faeries get excited when they smell peppermint. It is said to keep pests away, too.

The Middleworld—Earth

Cypress (*Cupressus sempervirens*)

Cypress essential oil is a wonderful essence. This tree species is over seventeen million years old. As an oil, it smells woody and brings the scent of a forest right into your home. It creates an aura of well-being and safety even when you are making a leap into new territory. This scent brings with it the flexibility and adaptability of these trees and what they have learned to do during the change of seasons. Faeries feel safe with the scent and are encouraged to reach out under its blanket of protection.

Vetiver (*Vetiveria zizanioides*)

Vetiver is a multitalented oil for relaxation and improved breathing. It is antiseptic and anti-inflammatory, and, after being diluted in a carrier oil, it can be applied to the skin for muscle soreness relief. Many humans use it for anxiety relief, increased alertness, and focus. It has excellent properties for repelling lice and insects. The Middleworld faeries love vetiver because the oil is extracted from the roots, making it earthy and comfortable for them.

Patchouli (*Pogostemon cablin*)

Patchouli boasts a deep, dark, thick, soothing essential oil. It is renowned for its uplifting, mood-enhancing qualities, and it possesses antimicrobial, anti-inflammatory, and antifungal properties. It is also an excellent insect repellent. It has been celebrated for bringing three forces of the body into balance: the creative center, the heart center, and the wisdom center. Patchouli is one of those essential oils we should have around at all times. The faeries love the harmony it brings to the body and the environment.

The Middleworld—Fire

Basil (*Ocimum basilicum*)

Basil is sometimes used to prepare holy water in some Greek Orthodox churches. Legend says it was found growing around Christ's tomb and was considered to be imbued with a divine essence. For that reason, it is revered by many faiths. Basil can sharpen the mind, relieve fatigue, and lessen the pain of sore muscles. It can help lift depression, melancholy, migraines, and nervous tension. Faeries believe this is a very special oil and treat it reverentially.

Clove (*Syzygium aromaticum*)

Clove is known as a "hot" oil because it is potent—it is among the most powerful of essential oils. Clove oil is a warming oil used for rheumatism, arthritis, digestive disorders, and wound healing. It is antiseptic and can tackle ailments like scabies, fungal infections, bruises, cuts, and scrapes. It repels fire ants and moths and has been known to be used by dentists to numb a sore tooth because it has anesthetic properties. Clove's aroma makes the body feel warm and cozy and aids in clearing the sinuses. Faeries use clove buds for cooking and for scenting their winter parties.

Cedarwood (*Cedrus atlantica, Cedrus deodara, Juniperus mexicana,* and *Juniperus virginiana*)

As you can see from the list of species, Cedar comes in many varieties: Atlas, Himalayan, Texan, and Virginian Cedarwood, respectively. The Cedars of Lebanon were used for building and ritual without being replanted, and so, after long being overharvested, they became extinct. The ancient Egyptians employed cedarwood oil for its antimicrobial and insecticidal properties and in the preparation for and preservation during mummification. Faeries like cedarwood because it has antiseptic properties that can be used for common injuries and wounds. It smells wonderful and can protect against bacterial infections.

Frankincense (*Boswellia carterri*)

Frankincense is a resin that comes from the sap of the Boswellia tree. It has anti-inflammatory, antiseptic, astringent, and wound healing properties. It increases the function of the immune system and helps with digestive system issues and discomforts. Many religions use frankincense in their rituals and services, elevating it to the level of sacred. It is a wonderful wrinkle inhibitor and can be used for relaxation and sensual indulgence. It was charred and ground into a black powder which was used as *kohl* eyeliner by the ancient Egyptians, in particular by the pharaoh Queen Hatshepsut. Faeries feel close to this essential oil because it is powerful and passionate.

Nutmeg (*Myristica fragrans*)

Nutmeg is another "hot" oil due to its warm, spicy nature. It has many medicinal benefits; it is an antioxidant and has properties that can reduce cellular damage and improve chronic conditions. It is antibacterial, anti-inflammatory, and anti-rheumatic. Nutmeg has been claimed to increase sexual libido in laboratory experiments, which is probably a secret the faeries have known all along. Its odor is warm and welcoming, especially in the cooler months when there is a chill in the air.

Orange (*Citrus sinensis*)

The fresh smell of sweet orange is enough to brighten anyone's day. This gorgeous essential oil is a spirit lifter and a joy enhancer and incites the instinct to dance. Orange creates the emotion of happiness because it is calming and brings a feeling of safety; it also has anti-inflammatory, antidepressant, antiseptic, and aphrodisiac effects. This essential oil can tick off a lot of boxes on the requirements for well-being and good mental health. No one can remain morose or blue when orange hits the air. It lifts one's mood by stimulating the lymphatic system and relaxes by reducing insomnia. Faeries are attracted to the joy of this aroma and delight in its presence.

The Lowerworld—Water

Blue Chamomile (*Matricaria chamomilla*)

Blue chamomile, also known as German chamomile, is a close sibling to Roman chamomile. It gets its blue color from *azulene*, a terpene found in the plant. It was used by Hippocrates, the father of modern medicine, for reducing fevers, motion sickness, and digestive complaints. Roman and Blue chamomile are both known as gentle oils, perfect for the elderly and children. They have anti-inflammatory, sedative, antibiotic, analgesic, antispasmodic, and antioxidant benefits. Chamomiles are known to reduce insomnia and promote a good night's sleep. Active faeries know they need their perfect rest.

Eucalyptus (*globulus*)

Eucalyptus was discovered in Australia by explorers in the eighteenth century. The Aborigines had been using it for centuries as an antiseptic because of its antiviral, antibacterial, antifungal, and antiviral properties. It is effective with respiratory infections, sinus issues, sore muscles, coughs, asthma, and for healing wounds, burns, cuts, and scrapes. There are many varieties of the eucalyptus species (five hundred), but *Eucalyptus globules* works just fine for most purposes. Faeries are enchanted by the smell and especially love it because it repels bothersome insects. Faeries prefer to repel rather than exterminate members of the insect family.

Jasmine (*Jasminum*)

With its floral scent, Jasmine may seem like it should be one of the aromas of the Upperworld, but it represents the Lowerworld of water because of its psychic and spiritual qualities. It uplifts the soul, carries a sense of calm to the deeper regions of the psyche, and balances the emotions, which are represented by the element of water. It even helps remove the signs of age, like wrinkles and sagging skin. Jasmine is a soothing friend to the inner world of human existence. The faeries love it because it is deep, secretive, and resides in the underworld with which they are most familiar and comfortable.

Essential Oils for Faeries

Myrrh (*Commiphora myrrha*)

The walls of Hatshepsut's tomb in ancient Egypt were decorated with carvings of Frankincense (*Boswellia*) and Myrrh (*Commiphora*) trees. The Egyptians imported myrrh from the south, where the Phoenicians sold it to them by the boatload in exchange for boatloads of gold. Both frankincense and myrrh were used in religious ceremonies for healing and for embalming and preserving the dead for the afterlife as mummies. Myrrh is a good insect repellent, perfume, wound salve, and rejuvenator for the skin. It is called Mo Yao in China, where it has been used for over one hundred conditions of the body. Myrrh is a sacred and special healer. For that reason and many more, the faeries love Myrrh and trust its abilities to help them.

Sandalwood (*Santalum album* and *Santalum spicatum*)

Sandalwood's nickname is "liquid gold" because it comes from the heartwood of the *Santalum album* tree. The medicinal properties of this oil are astringent, stimulant, disinfectant, antibacterial, antiviral, and antitumoral. It provides grounding and stability as well as remedies for viral infections and skin issues including cold sores and herpes simplex. Indian sandalwood (*Santalum album*), a now-protected species, was the original source, so these days, most sandalwood oil comes from *Santalum spicatum*, which is an Australian sandalwood tree. The sandalwood scent is said to transform one's material desires into spiritual goals. It assists in meditation, inner processes, and spiritual maturation. The faeries love to make connections to the higher realms using the energies of the Lowerworld to reach it.

Bergamot (*Citrus bergamia*)

The enchanting fragrance of Bergamot is either a scent you love or not. It is extracted from the rind of a green-colored citrus fruit and is also used to flavor Earl Grey Tea, which the faeries enjoy for their afternoon tea parties. It is analgesic, antiseptic, antidepressant, deodorant, antibiotic, and sedative. All those qualities in one little oil!

Faeries consider essential oils to be mini pharmacies in a bottle. Each essential oil has qualities that can help them live healthier and happier lives. The difference is they have known this for millennia, and we're just getting started.

You can certainly incorporate other essential oils into your work and friendship with faeries. I have suggested ones that connect to them via the three realms. The very fact that you elect to scent the air when you contact the faery world is extremely flattering to them. Besides being a lovely thing to do, the scents will help to connect you to these special places and make your bond to the faery world even stronger and more magical. Use the ceremonies I have laid out in Chapter 7 and see for yourself how well the natural elements flow together and make for an engaging and uplifting experience with the faeries.

CHAPTER ELEVEN

How Will You Know a Faery Has Come to Visit?

Some of the very first signs you will notice if a faery comes to call is that you might hear the most beautiful music with the most exquisite melody and be uplifted by the sound. You may notice that everything in your garden is blooming, ablaze with color, birds, and bees and that they all exude vibrant health. You may suddenly feel like laughing or giggling, and your whole being might feel lighter. You may walk with a new spring in your step. You may feel like breaking into dance for no reason at all. When you look up at the sky, you may see sparkles and apparitions of faery folk.

All of the above are sure signs that the faeries are exploring you and may decide to park their faerymobiles in your garage. They would have to call a large council meeting of all the elders to determine if this is a safe place for them or not. They will set out little tests for you, and if you pass, they may very well become your neighbors.

They will test you to see if you really believe in magic. They may send sprinkles of faery dust and glitter into your life. They may speak to you through animals; they may entice you into games so that you don't act your age; they may cause you to paint or to sing a tune you've never heard of before, and they could send you flashes of light at the strangest of times. You may find yourself feeling what animals feel, deepening your connection and love of Mother Nature, having magical dreams that you remember the next day, and living with a feeling that someone or something wonderful is watching over you.

Things may appear and disappear, animals may suddenly become attracted to you and will stop to communicate with you, birds will flock to your yard and share their songs with you, and you will feel cheerful and ready to greet the day with a smile, loving the world in a way you have never done before.

You may become more passionate than you have previously about the environment and protecting the planet. You may feel yourself surrounded by a blanket of warmth and comfort; you may feel enhanced creativity in your work and play; and you may be led down new paths and attracted to realms you never knew existed before.

There are a few things you can do to keep the faeries happy while they are in your territory: keep a tidy home free of clutter with room for light, air, and dancing; read more about magic and magical things; show gratitude and respect for the presence of a faery; greet every living thing as though it is a faery.

You just never know when you may be entertaining a visiting faery. Keep your spirits high, your attitude positive, and your mind centered on possibilities. Be polite, use kindness to open doors, handle Mother Nature as if you were a guest in her garden, speak the truth, and remain honest in your heart and soul. Encourage children to believe in faeries, our kind of faeries, and tell them magic is real.

Make a list of things you would like to ask a faery, should you have the opportunity to meet one in person. Here are some thoughts to get you started on your list.

- How can faery magic help you? (Remember you have to ask three times.)

- What gifts do you want from the faeries? What can you offer in return?

- Faeries come in all colors, all sexes, and all nationalities, but they all speak Fey.

- Using magic, they can speak to anyone in their native tongue if they choose to.

- Will faeries teach me to speak Fey if I ask three times?

- Will they teach me magic?

- How will you create boundaries for your faery friends?

- How do I know if I might be a faery?

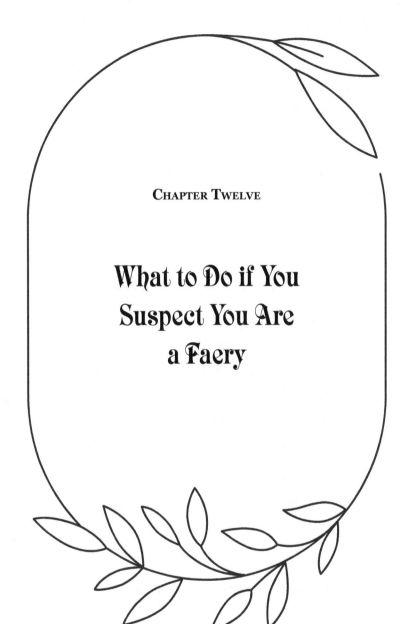

CHAPTER TWELVE

What to Do if You Suspect You Are a Faery

Many people in the world feel like they have come from another planet, another dimension, or another world. It's not unusual and it may be correct. Not everyone comes from the same place, as the ancients knew only too well and as we are just beginning to accept in our time. If you are one of those beings who feels you may be from someplace else or has otherworldly tendencies and talents, you probably are. Why not explore that feeling and find out if you are from another place and time? For example, you might be a faery in a human suit.

You'll know you are a faery if you:

- Dream of faeries and mystical beings.

- Have a deep, abiding connection with nature.

- Do not feel obligated to act your age.

- Are spontaneous and fluid about life.

- Possess creative abilities like painting, singing, dancing, writing and expression.

- Find it is easy to communicate with animals.

- Love to laugh and find humor in the simple things.

- Feel like there are beings always around you.

- Have an attraction to things that sparkle and flash.

- Present a cheerful face to the world.

- Feel joy every day.

- Read books about mystical and magical people and things.

- Resonate and feel at home with the elements of air, earth, fire, and water.

- Sense that you hear faeries talking to you. You catch a few words now and then.

- Never, ever question magic.

- Love spending time in a garden.

- Could never harm anyone or anything.

- When you wish upon a star, you do it three times.

So what if you qualify? Would it be scary to discover that you are a faery or have faery tendencies? Maybe you are. Here are guidelines written by the incredibly talented Anam Cara Cat. She outlines what it takes to be a faery. With her kind permission, here is the inspirational piece:

How to Be a Fairy

Believe you are one
Invite magic into your life
Create your own enchanting wings
Always use your powers for good
Design your own reality full of happiness, peace, and love
Celebrate every day with laughter, songs, and play
Paint sunrises on rocks and leave them on empty doorsteps
Picnic with a grasshopper and unravel the mysteries of
the universe
Plant your favorite cookie crumbs for the ants
Grow a wish garden and bring your dreams to life one by one
Blow kisses to gray clouds and paint your toenails
with raindrops
Build elegant butterfly houses and rent them out for free
Find something beautiful in everyone you meet and remind
them of it

Dance Daily

Hug trees until you can feel a heart beating with yours

Share your secrets with our feathered and furry friends

Follow rainbows with kindred spirits and discover the treasures along the way

Fill empty spaces with flowers

Whisper your worries to dragonflies and let them be carried far, far away

Write poems about friendship, faith, and forgiveness and leave them on park benches

Nap in the grass and let ladybugs dance in your hair

Stretch time and space and travel to new lands

Explore the wonder of you

Soak your soul in sunsets—Twilight is a fairy's finest hour

Listen to the quiet

Attend cricket symphonies by moonlight

Make wishes for other people on shooting stars

Let your wings carry you where no one else has been and light the way for others to follow

Spread the message: Everything is possible!

Remember, when you believe in yourself, you inspire others to do the same.

Written by Anam Cara Cat. A full-color poster of these beautiful words is available at: anamcaracat.com/products/how-to-be-a-fairy-poster

Conclusion

Faeries bring out the positive facets of yourself. They provide a stunning world of success where there may have previously been lack. They leave sparkle behind wherever they go. The world is always made better when a faery passes through it and leaves reminders for us that there is powerful magic all around. Faeries keep the wonder alive and nurture the creative bones of each person who believes in them. Never allow the winds of doubt to carry your talents away.

Nurture the gifts the faeries bring you and enhance them through peaceful living, kind interactions, and music. If you see a rainbow, stop what you're doing in order to acknowledge its spectacular beauty and sense deep in your heart that a faery is behind the wondrous display of color, beauty, and magnificence. The goal of faeries is to show us there is no separation between the worlds and that we truly are all one: humans, animals, plants, stones, and faeries alike. We live and exist compatibly in multiple dimensions throughout the universe.

When you live your life with the faeries, invite them in, and live in accordance with their soulful spirituality and in alignment with faery precepts, you will become infused with the energy of the spirits, elements, and creation and your life will unfold like a poem. It will turn out to be the best life you could possibly ever live.

Acknowledgments

Every writer needs a muse. I am blessed with a muse, editor, cheerleader, and faery-lover all rolled into one. Marlene Morris has been all that and more during the writing of this book. Her continuous support, endless editing, and positive influence have brought this work to fruition. My deepest gratitude to her for her belief in me *and* my faeries.

Another debt of gratitude goes to Pamela Ventura, my sister-in-law, who is always there to lend a kind word and cheerful astonishment at whatever is coming out of my hard drive. Her positive support and squeals of laughter are worth their weight in gold.

Special thanks to Brenda Knight for asking me to write this book for Mango Media and to Ron Schultz, Obi-Ron, not to be confused with Oberon, for the introduction to Mango Publishing and his support of my literary endeavors.

Thank you to Cat (Anam Cara Cat) for allowing me to include her beautiful words, "How to Be a Fairy."

Thank you to Lisa Hagan, my amazing agent, who is in my corner no matter what, brave and courageous soul that she is. Thanks to Lisa Tenzin-Dolma, J. Randy, and Spencer Taraborrelli for their continuous good cheer and astonishing excellence in achievement, to David Bruner for his love and support of elves and Harry Potter, and to Don Burgess, who could and would happily design and build the most fantastical Faeryland ever seen. Carolyn Lombardo deserves special acknowledgment for her appreciation of the spirits in the

Kappa Kappa Gamma house, and appreciation to Mandy Rose for living with us for fourteen years and bringing her faery friends into the house every chance she got.

Finally, I want to thank the forests, woods, meadows, mounds, burrows, stone monuments, gardens, hills, and dales in the USA, Ireland, and the UK that have brought the faery spirits forth for me to meet and befriend.

And, of course, thank you to all the faery folk for making my dreams come true.

Addendum A

The IMDB website lists twenty-seven films as having faery content: *Pinocchio* and *Fantasia* (1940), *Cinderella* (1950), *Peter Pan* (1953), *Sleeping* Beauty (1959), *Legend* (1985), *Fairy Tale: A True Story* (1997), *Wonderful World of Disney* and *Toothless* (1997), *The Magical Legend of the Leprechauns* (1999), *A Midsummer Night's Dream* (1999), *The 10th Kingdom* (2000), *Moulin Rouge* and *A.I. Artificial Intelligence* (2001), *Darkness Falls* (2003), *Peter Pan* (2003), *Tooth, Ella Enchanted*, and *Shrek 2* (2004), *Tooth Fairy* (2006), *The Santa Clause 3: The Escape Clause* (2006), *Tinker Belle* (2008), *Tooth Fairy II* (2010), and *Neverland* in (2011).

Reference Sources

Know your Celtic Tree Astrology (based on birth date):
blog.fantasticgardeners.co.uk/whats-your-tree-sign-according-to-celtic-tree-astrology

Know your flower sign:
blog.fantasticgardeners.co.uk/what-flower-matches-your-star-sign

Learn the herbs connected to your astrological sign:
www.thespruce.com/herbs-corresponding-to-horoscope-1762360

How to Be a Fairy Poster by Anam Cara Cat:
anamcaracat.com/products/how-to-be-a-fairy-poster

Bibliography

Anderson, Rosemarie. *Celtic Oracles, A New System for Spiritual Growth and Divination.* New York: Harmony Books, 1998.

Blamires, Steve. *Glamoury, Magic of the Celtic Green World.* St. Paul, MN: Llewellyn Publications, 2000.

Briggs, Katharine Mary. *An Encyclopedia of Fairies*, p. xi. New York: Pantheon Books, 1997.

Castleden, Rodney. *The Element Encyclopedia of the Celts.* United Kingdom: Harper Element, 2012.

Criswell, Colleen. *The Magical Circle School Newsletter.* 8 2015. www.amazon.com/Crystal-Crazy-HCI-1015-Jasper-Sphere/dp/B00NIG5PTY (accessed October 5, 2018).

Hope, Murry. *Practical Egyptian Magic.* New York: St. Martin's Press, 1984.

Kendall, Paul. "Trees for Life Rowan Mythology." *Trees for Life Rewilding the Scottish Highlands.* 2020. treesforlife. org.uk/into-the-forest/trees-plants-animals/trees/rowan/ rowan-mythology-and-folklore/ (accessed June 4, 2020).

MacEowen, Frank. *The Spiral of Memory and Belonging.* Novato, CA: New World Library, 2004.

MacKenzie, Donald A. "Chapter IV, Demons, Fairies and Ghosts." *Sacred-Texts.com.* 1915. www.sacred-texts.com/ ane/mba/mba10.htm (accessed May 15, 2020).

Nace, Trevor. *Forbes.* June 13, 2018. www.forbes.com/sites/
    trevornace/2018/06/13/hawaiis-volcano-is-literally-
    erupting-gems/#1f4d906725da (accessed June 12, 2020).

Pöldinger, W. "Pubmed.ncbi.nlm.nih.gov/." *PubMed.gov.* 12
    14, 2000. pubmed.ncbi.nlm.nih.gov/11155493/ (accessed
    June 13, 2020).

Young, Kac. *Crystal Power: 12 Essential Crystals for Health &
    Healing.* Woodbury, MN: Llewellyn, 2020.

—. *The Healing Art of Essential Oils.* Woodbury, MN:
    Llewellyn Publications, 2017.

About the Author

Kac Young has earned three doctorates: a PhD in Natural Health, an ND in Naturopathy, and a DCH in Clinical Hypnotherapy. She is also a licensed Religious Science Minister. An active television professional for over thirty years, she has won awards for producing and directing. She was also a studio executive for Universal and is a consultant and advisor to many Hollywood-industry companies, studios, and stars.

Kac has traveled extensively to experience firsthand and study world religions, beliefs, methods, practices, and disciplines. Her life goal is to bring spiritual awareness to everyone, so they can live full, productive, generous lives and leave the world a better place for having been in it. She believes that every human desire must be spiritually connected and consciously infused for change to transpire. When desire and intention meet passion and action, shift occurs. When shift occurs; change happens, and the desired results are experienced.

To date she has written twenty-three self-help books: *Heart Easy: The Food Lover's Guide to Heart Healthy Eating*, *Discover Your Spiritual Genius*, *Feng Shui the Easy Way*, *Dancing with the Moon*, *21 Days to the Love of Your Life*, *Gold Mind*, *Cheese Dome Power*, *The Path to Fabulous*, *The*

Quick Guide to Bach Flower Remedies, Supreme Healing, The Enlightened Person's Guide to Raising a Dog, Chart Your Course, The Healing Art of Essential Oils, Essential Oils for Beginners, The One-Minute Cat Manager, Natural Healing for Cats Combining Bach Flower Remedies and Behavior Therapy, Crystals Power, the Twelve Essential Crystal for Health and Healing, The Art of Healing with Crystals, Pendulum Power Wisdom and Healing, and the annual *Essential Oils Wall Calendar* for Llewellyn Publishing 2020, 2021 and 2022.

About the Author

Mango Publishing, established in 2014, publishes an eclectic list of books by diverse authors—both new and established voices—on topics ranging from business, personal growth, women's empowerment, LGBTQ studies, health, and spirituality to history, popular culture, time management, decluttering, lifestyle, mental wellness, aging, and sustainable living. We were recently named 2019 *and* 2020's #1 fastest growing independent publisher by *Publishers Weekly.* Our success is driven by our main goal, which is to publish high quality books that will entertain readers as well as make a positive difference in their lives.

Our readers are our most important resource; we value your input, suggestions, and ideas. We'd love to hear from you—after all, we are publishing books for you!

Please stay in touch with us and follow us at:

Facebook: Mango Publishing
Twitter: @MangoPublishing
Instagram: @MangoPublishing
LinkedIn: Mango Publishing
Pinterest: Mango Publishing
Newsletter: mangopublishinggroup.com/newsletter

Join us on Mango's journey to reinvent publishing, one book at a time.

CPSIA information can be obtained
at www.ICGtesting.com
Printed in the USA
LVHW021339300121
677872LV00006B/6

9 781642 500615